TO AT-RISK ANIMALS EVERYWHERE:
WE CARE.
WE'RE SORRY.
WE'RE TRYING.

Published in the UK by Scholastic Children's Books, 2021
Euston House, 24 Eversholt Street, London, NW1 1DB
A division of Scholastic Ltd

London ~ New York ~ Toronto ~ Sydney ~ Auckland
Mexico City ~ New Delhi ~ Hong Kong

SCHOLASTIC and associated logos are trademarks and/or
registered trademarks of Scholastic Inc.

Published in the UK by Scholastic Ltd, 2021

Text copyright © Kimberlie Hamilton 2021

Illustrations © Scholastic Children's Books, 2021

Cover illustration by Aaron Cushley
Inside illustrations by Emma Jayne, Jestenia Southerland, Kim Ekdahl, Tsai-Yi Huang, Amelia
Herbertson, Steph Marshall, Stephanie Fizer Coleman, Juliana Motzko and Katie Wilson.
Images of Sammy Jo, Elsa and Scout by Sarah Kathryn Bean (P.145).

The right of Kimberlie Hamilton to be identified as the author of this work has been asserted by her in
accordance with the Copyright, Designs and Patents Act, 1988.

ISBN 978 0702 30011 0

Printed in China
Papers used by Scholastic Children's Books are made from wood grown in sustainable forests.

2 4 6 8 10 9 7 5 3 1

www.scholastic.co.uk

REBEL Animals AT RISK

STORIES OF SURVIVAL

BY KIMBERLIE HAMILTON

With illustrators from
around the world...

ILLUSTRATIONS BY: AARON CUSHLEY, EMMA JAYNE, JESTENIA SOUTHERLAND, KIM EKDAHL, TSAI-YI HUANG, AMELIA HERBERTSON, STEPH MARSHALL, STEPHANIE FIZER COLEMAN, JULIANA MOTZKO AND KATIE WILSON

■SCHOLASTIC

CONTENTS

AT-RISK ANIMALS NEED OUR HELP!

Our planet is home to all sorts of amazing animals, from tiny hummingbirds to whales longer than two double-decker buses. Yet many of these animals are in trouble. Some species that once roamed the earth in great numbers are now gone for ever. And like the dinosaurs of long ago, many animals today are on the edge of extinction.

The cause of this mass extinction? Us. HUMANS.

The good news is that we humans also have the power to turn things around. We can change the future of the world and its animals by taking positive action. But we'd better hurry. Many species featured in this book are classified as endangered, and the others could easily find themselves in the same situation.

As individuals, all of these animals are "rebels" for being survivors, making history or doing something memorable or unexpected. Hopefully getting to know their stories will inspire young naturalists, eco-activists and animal lovers (like you!) to find out how to help animals like them.

READY TO START?
IF SO, KEEP READING...

THE RED LIST

Believe it or not, 99.9 per cent of species that have ever existed on earth are no longer here. Many scientists think we are in the middle of a mass extinction, a time when huge numbers of living things will die out.

To help pinpoint which species need the most help, the International Union for Conservation of Nature (IUCN) created a list of at-risk animals. The IUCN Red List currently features over 30,000 mammals, birds and amphibians. Of these, more than a quarter are in danger of extinction.

Wildlife experts assign each animal on the list to a specific category:

🐾 **LEAST CONCERN:**
Widespread and in no danger of soon becoming extinct

🐾 **NEAR THREATENED:**
Could be in trouble soon

ENDANGERED

VULNERABLE

EXTINCT

🐾 **VULNERABLE:**
Facing a high risk of extinction in the wild

🐾 **ENDANGERED:**
Facing a very high risk of extinction in the wild

🐾 **CRITICALLY ENDANGERED:**
Facing an extremely high risk of extinction in the wild

🐾 **EXTINCT IN THE WILD:**
Only found in zoos or captive breeding programmes

🐾 **EXTINCT:**
No longer found in the wild, in captivity or in captive breeding programmes

The Red List covers only the species the IUCN has assessed so far, which is just a fraction of the animals we know about. There are countless more species out there yet to be discovered!

AFRICA

When we think of Africa, images of elephants, giraffes and zebras strolling the plains and gorillas on forested hillsides often come to mind. Most of us have only met these creatures in books and films and on visits to zoos. But with many African animals under threat, it's time to make sure these are not the only places to find them in the future.

As hard as it is to believe, some people deliberately kill these wild animals. They might be poachers seeking to sell body parts, or hunters who do it as a twisted form of fun. Shockingly, this cruel "sport" is still happening around the world despite action by conservationists and activists.

Cecil the lion was one of the most famous big cats on the continent and a well-known research subject. When a trophy hunter killed him in 2015, people were shocked and angry. Despite the outrage over Cecil's death, hunters are still allowed to kill lions in many parts of Africa. There are laws against poaching animals such as rhinos and elephants, yet it still happens because their horns and tusks can be sold for enormous sums of money.

African wildlife faces other dangers besides poaching. Baby chimps are stolen and sold as exotic pets. Mountain gorillas are killed for bushmeat and eaten by humans. Giraffes are facing a "silent extinction" that much of the world doesn't even know about. The list goes on and on.

The animals that share our planet exist together in a delicate balance. Scientists have discovered that the decline or disappearance of just a single species can have a negative impact on many others. This is why it is so important to help all of Africa's wonderful wildlife.

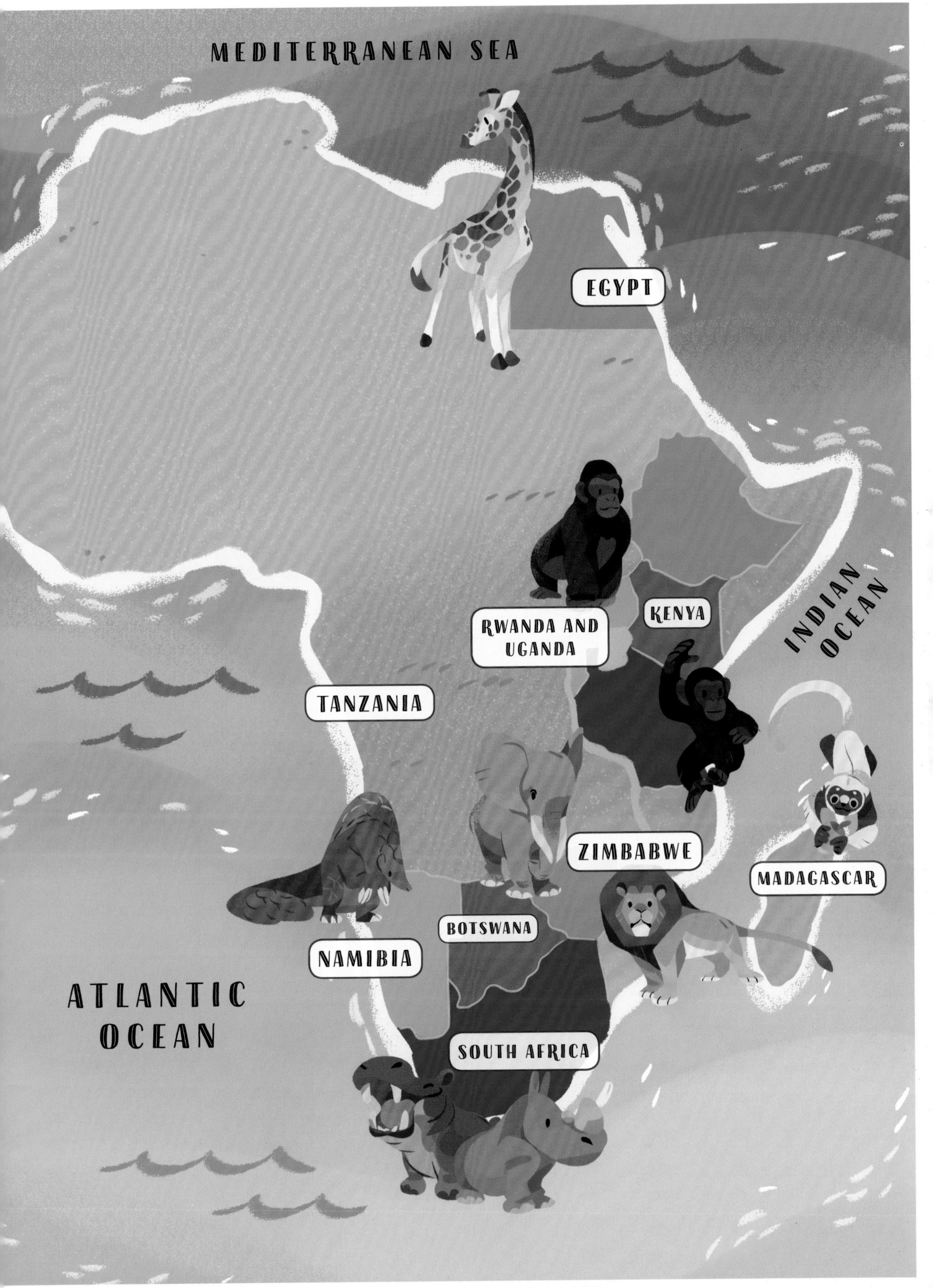

MEDITERRANEAN SEA

EGYPT

RWANDA AND UGANDA

KENYA

INDIAN OCEAN

TANZANIA

ZIMBABWE

MADAGASCAR

NAMIBIA

BOTSWANA

ATLANTIC OCEAN

SOUTH AFRICA

AYUMU CHIMPANZEE

Ayumu is a chimp who is a memory champ. His short-term memory is better than that of most humans. In the blink of an eye, he can remember the exact position of nine numbers randomly flashed up on a computer screen. In one test, he not only outscored other chimpanzees, he trounced a group of red-faced university students! The Japanese professor who studies him describes Ayumu as "naughty but harder working" than the other young primates in his research lab. Yet Ayumu's uncanny ability to recall images he's seen for just a fraction of a second is not a skill that can be learned – it's just how his brain naturally works. This means that animals can not only be faster and stronger than humans, they sometimes can be a lot smarter than us too.

ECHO ELEPHANT

With crossed tusks that made her easy to recognize, Echo was the matriarch of the world's most studied elephant family. She lived in a wildlife reserve in Kenya and was featured in books and documentaries. One film-making team followed Echo and her closest relatives for decades, recording every aspect of their lives. They observed elephants displaying a wide range of emotions, including comforting each other when distressed and grieving when one of their family members died. The team even filmed Echo giving birth, an event rarely captured on camera. Other memorable moments included Echo's dramatic rescue of a baby elephant who had been kidnapped by a rival family! Echo died in her sixties in 2009, but in true elephant fashion, she will never be forgotten.

HONEY BUN PANGOLIN

Honey Bun looks like a tiny dinosaur covered with sharp brown scales. This body armour is the reason pangolins around the world have been hunted to the point of extinction, as their scales are used in traditional Chinese medicine. Thankfully, Honey Bun is safe from harm at a sanctuary in Namibia. She became known after starring in the BBC wildlife documentary *Pangolins: The World's Most Wanted Animal*. Honey Bun also appeared in a video campaign for pangolins with Chinese superstar Angelababy, which was seen by more than 25 million viewers in China the day it was released. Getting people to care about pangolins is of utmost importance for their survival, and Honey Bun is doing a fantastic job as an ambassador for her species.

HUBERTA HIPPOPOTAMUS

Huberta the "wandering hippo" is one of the most famous animals in South African history. She set out on a walk in 1928 and just kept going. She made her way south along the coastline, tramping through gardens and sugar-cane fields, crossing rivers and golf courses, and venturing places few hippos had ever gone before. Local villagers gave Huberta a warm welcome wherever she went, believing that she brought them luck. Nothing got in her way – not even the noise and traffic of a big city, where she strolled right down the middle of a busy street. Was she visiting ancestral lands? Searching for an old buddy? No one will ever know. All in all, she walked 1,600 kilometres (1,000 miles) during a remarkable three-year journey that captured the hearts of the African people.

JOVIAN LEMUR

Jovian was the star of the American TV show *Zoboomafoo*, a popular wildlife programme for kids. During the show's 65-episode run, the white-furred, yellow-eyed lemur delighted schoolchildren around the world with his silly antics. He was bouncy and playful, loved to snack on mangoes and garbanzo beans, and could be quite naughty too – he couldn't resist grabbing the noses of his human friends. Jovian retired to a lemur centre in North Carolina, USA, where the loveable long-limbed lemur fathered twelve babies and attracted thousands of visitors a year. He introduced scores of people to lemurs, primates that are found in the wild in only one place on earth – Madagascar, a tropical island off the east coast of Africa.

KOKO GORILLA

Koko was born in 1971 at a zoo in California, USA, and became famous for understanding more than 2,000 words of spoken English and 1,000 words in a version of American Sign Language. She had a cheeky sense of humour and one of the first signs she used to describe herself was "queen". Koko was the star of several documentaries and counted comedian Robin Williams among her many celebrity friends. She was a talented photographer and one image she took of her own reflection in a mirror was even used on the cover of *National Geographic*. Another time, the magazine featured an adorable cover photo of Koko cuddling a kitten she had requested for her birthday. A gentle giant, Koko was admired by millions and changed the way many people thought about gorillas.

SUDAN RHINOCEROS

With their unique horns, rhinos have been called "chubby unicorns", but they rarely live fairy-tale lives. Rhinos are targeted by poachers for their horns, which can be illegally sold for a great deal of money. Sudan spent nearly 35 years at a European zoo, where he was safe from harm, but he did not manage to breed. This was a big problem because Sudan was one of only four northern white rhinos left on earth, and if he failed to reproduce his species would become extinct. Conservationists came up with a crazy plan to airlift Sudan and the other rhinos to Kenya, hoping their native habitat might inspire them to mate. Surrounded by armed guards night and day, Sudan thrived in Africa and fathered a daughter. The world mourned when he died in 2018 – the last male of his kind.

ZARAFA GIRAFFE

Zarafa was just a baby when she was captured in Egypt, Africa in 1825, destined to be a gift for the king of France. Loaded on board a ship, she sailed down the Nile and across the Mediterranean to France, her head poking through a hole in the ship's deck. Upon reaching land, she began an epic 885-kilometre (550-mile) walk from Marseille to Paris accompanied by a famous naturalist, Geoffroy Saint-Hilaire. Crowds of spectators lined her path for the entire 40-day journey, eager to see the exotic, long-lashed creature with their very own eyes. Zarafa arrived in Paris in 1827, where she nibbled rose petals from King Charles X's hand and went to live at the Jardin des Plantes. With her beautiful long neck, Zarafa kicked off a giraffe-themed cultural craze that lasted 18 years, inspiring everything from art to textiles to ladies' hair styles that were shaped like tall horns!

AFRICAN WILDLIFE WINS

Animals and humans are working together in inventive ways to save threatened species in Africa:

- An anti-poaching hound called K9 Killer is South Africa's top dog in the fight against illegal rhino-hunting. The Belgian Malinois was awarded a PDSA Gold Medal for his bravery and devotion to duty.

- Only two northern white rhinos now remain: Sudan's daughter and granddaughter, Najin and Fatu. Scientists hope that a high-tech captive breeding programme using IVF can save the species.

- Now that many countries have banned the sale of elephant ivory, the next goal is to stop the demand. Celebrities and other influencers are helping spread the message that buying ivory is wrong.

- Former shelter pups are being trained as conservation dogs to help scientists track gorillas through their dense forest habitat. They do it by following the scent of the apes' poo!

- Mountain gorillas are back from the brink of extinction thanks to eco-tourism. Adventure-seekers pay hefty fees to go gorilla trekking in

Rwanda and Uganda, funding conservation programmes and proving that the apes are worth more money alive than dead.

- "Pangolin men" at wildlife sanctuaries are helping save the scaly little anteaters by acting as their bodyguards. The men walk with the pangolins as they forage for food, protecting them from poachers.

- Four retired racehorses are helping protect rhinos from poachers at a private game reserve in South Africa. The horses are very alert and their size and speed helps to deter poachers while not disturbing the rhinos.

- Rothschild's giraffes that live in the grounds of Giraffe Manor in Kenya often surprise hotel guests by poking their heads through the windows. Such up-close encounters with animals are an excellent way to get tourists interested in conservation projects.

- The Aspinall Foundation embarked on a secret mission to dehorn hundreds of rhinos in 2020 to prevent them being killed by poachers. The horns are made of keratin, like human hair and fingernails, so the rhinos are not hurt, and the horns grow back within three years.

- Endangered pangolins have new and unexpected allies – specially trained rats that can sniff out illegal shipments of pangolin scales.

OTHER AMAZING AFRICAN ANIMALS

ALEX was an African grey parrot who could count, identify different shapes and use more than a hundred words. He is the only non-human animal to ever ask a question about himself. Gazing in a mirror, he wanted to know what colour he was.

BINTI JUA was a female gorilla who made worldwide headlines in 1996 when she gently carried a boy to safety after he fell into a primate enclosure at a zoo in Chicago, USA.

DAVID GREYBEARD was Dr Jane Goodall's favourite chimp, the first who trusted her and the first she observed using tools. This was something scientists once thought only humans were smart enough to do. *Time* magazine named David one of history's 15 most influential animals.

ELSA was an orphaned lion cub adopted by a game warden and his wife in Kenya in the 1950s. They taught her how to survive on her own and later released her into the wild. A popular book about her life, *Born Free*, introduced readers to wildlife conservation and was made into a film.

HAM the "astrochimp" became the first chimpanzee to survive a trip to outer space in 1961. Many people now believe it's wrong to subject animals to such an ordeal, but Ham will always be remembered for what he did for the sake of science.

JONATHAN the Seychelles giant tortoise was born in 1832 and is thought to be the oldest living land animal in the world.

OWEN was an orphaned baby hippo who was best buddies with a 130-year-old giant tortoise named **MZEE**. They lived together at a sanctuary in Kenya and formed an unlikely friendship.

SHIRLEY AND JENNY were two elephants who were overjoyed to be reunited at an animal sanctuary in Tennessee, USA in 1999. They'd met briefly decades earlier but still remembered each other, proving the old saying that "elephants never forget".

STOFFEL was a determined honey badger who made headlines for his repeated escapes from a wildlife rehabilitation centre in South Africa. He also visited a local lodge, where he chased the staff out of the kitchen and helped himself to some tasty food.

ANTARCTICA AND THE ARCTIC
THE POLES

The Antarctic and Arctic are two of the coldest and most remote places on earth. Most people can't imagine living in such extreme conditions, yet there are many animals that have made these icy realms their home.

Polar bears, for example, are one of the best-known species that thrive in the ice and snow of the Arctic. Unfortunately, climate change has taken a toll on the planet's polar regions, and polar bears are now famous for a different reason — they've become a symbol of endangered species.

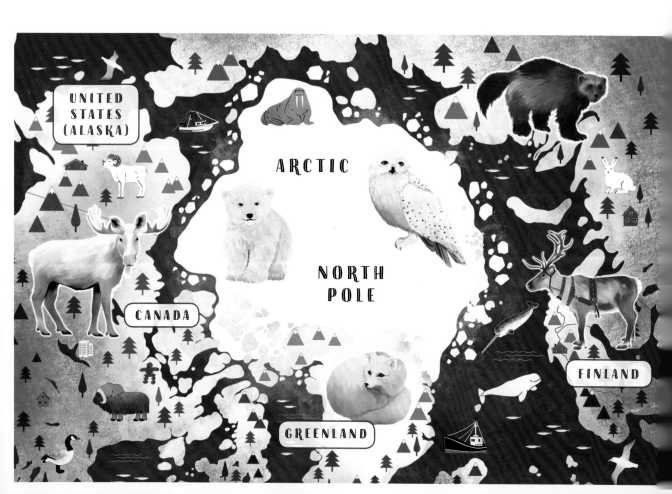

Antarctica and the Arctic are warming twice as fast as other parts of the world and that's causing the ice to melt and sea levels to rise. Experts say the Arctic is actually heating up at *least* twice as fast as the rest of the planet. In 2019, one polar researcher in Greenland was so shocked to see the visibly shrinking ice sheet that he took a photo of his sled dog team wading through ankle-deep water. The photo later went viral on social media.

Melting ice and rising seas are bad news for the wildlife living in polar regions. Climate change is already affecting animals all over the world, but species in the Arctic and Antarctic cannot move to a colder spot. Polar bears need the sea ice to hunt, raise their young and rest after long periods of swimming. Seals make caves in the snow and ice to raise their pups, feed and mate. If their habitat continues to disappear, these and many other polar animals will have no other place to go.

BRUMAS POLAR BEAR

Brumas was born in London Zoo in 1949. She was mistakenly thought to be a boy at first and named after her keepers, Bruce and Sam. The roly-poly cub was an instant hit, and the British public simply couldn't get enough of her. People waited in long queues each day just to catch a glimpse of the snow-white furball. Prince Charles of the British royal family – still a young cub himself at the time – also paid her a visit. Zookeepers actually paraded Brumas around the grounds in a baby buggy, something that would be a big no-no today. She was the first polar bear to grow up at the zoo, an achievement celebrated with books, postcards and cuddly toys. Most astonishing of all, Brumas is credited with boosting zoo attendance from one to three million visitors a year.

THE FLEET-FOOTED FOX ARCTIC FOX

An Arctic fox gained fame for walking from Norway across Greenland to Canada in just 76 days. At more than 3,500 kilometres (2,200 miles), it was the longest journey ever recorded for the species. Astounded researchers following the fox's progress in 2019 wondered if she'd been taken on board a boat. As it turned out, the clever fox had used sea ice to get to where she was going. She travelled about 46 kilometres (29 miles) a day, and one day she went an astonishing 155 kilometres (97 miles), setting a new speed record. It was the first time scientists had documented the movement of foxes between continents and their findings raised concerns about the future impact of climate change. The fox's tracker eventually stopped working but hopefully she's still on the move, somewhere!

GIZMO SNOWY OWL

In the popular Harry Potter books, owls deliver letters and parcels to the students at Hogwarts School of Witchcraft and Wizardry. Harry's feathered friend, Hedwig, is a beautiful snowy owl. In two of the films, *Harry Potter and the Philosopher's Stone* and *Harry Potter and the Chamber of Secrets*, an owl named Gizmo was the main animal actor who played the role of Hedwig. Hedwig is a female character but Gizmo was a boy – that's because male snowies are whiter and smaller than females and were easier for the child actors to hold. Gizmo's performance introduced snowy owls to legions of Potter fans, boosting much-needed awareness for a polar species that needs our help to survive.

GRUMPY REINDEER

Grumpy played a central role in the 2015 television documentary *Reindeer Family & Me*. The film focused on the nomadic Sami people of Finnish Lapland and their herds of reindeer. The Sami don't give their animals names, but BBC cameraman Gordon Buchanan jokingly nicknamed one of them "Grumpy". Attitude aside, the reindeer became a trusty guide on Gordon's solo journey through the sub-Arctic landscape and even posed with him for selfies as the Northern Lights shimmered overhead. Grumpy proved to have superb instincts too. At one point, he stopped dead in his tracks at a frozen lake and refused to budge. Gordon stepped off the sled and his foot nearly plunged through the thin ice. Grumpy had somehow sensed the danger and saved his human companion's life!

M56 WOLVERINE

Aside from a certain Marvel comic book character, M56 may be the most famous wolverine ever. Wolverines are native to the Arctic but M56 made his home in North America. In 2008, scientists fitted him with a radio collar to track his movements. Over the next eight years, he travelled hundreds of kilometres over tough terrain in Wyoming, Colorado, Montana and North Dakota. He brought so much attention to the struggles of wolverines that the idea of reintroducing the species began to be developed by specialists. M56's tracker stopped working in 2012, but hikers and rangers kept a watchful eye out for him until he passed away four years later. In his honour, conservationists continue to fight to get wolverines the legal protections they need to survive.

RONNIE AND REGGIE PENGUINS

London Zoo is home to two famous gay penguins named Ronnie and Reggie. The duo made headlines when they adopted an egg that had been abandoned by another couple. Ronnie and Reggie shared parenting duties until their chick was able to strike out on his own. Same-sex couples are very common in the animal kingdom – in fact, they are so commonplace that the zoo hosted its very own Penguin Pride Parade in 2019, inspired by London's annual LGBT+ parade for humans. To announce the big event, Ronnie and Reggie posed for photos next to a banner bearing the slogan, "Some penguins are gay, get over it." The couple's devotion has been an eye-opener for many zoo visitors, showing that animals' closest relationships are as important to them as ours are to us.

VOYAGER ARCTIC TERN

A tiny Arctic tern set a world record for the longest migratory flight in 2016. The adventurous tern doesn't have a proper name but, following her epic journey, "Voyager" is very fitting. Researchers tagged the bird with a tracking device before she set off from her breeding grounds in the Farne Islands, off the coast of northern England. She reached the tip of South Africa one month later, then cruised over the Indian Ocean and down to Antarctica. She stayed on the move constantly, flying day and night. It remains a mystery how migratory birds find the energy to go such incredible distances. By the time she returned home to the UK, the tern's exhausting journey added up to nearly 96,000 kilometres (60,000 miles). That's equal to flying around the planet twice!

WHITE MOOSE MOOSE

White Moose was an albino moose who once roamed the forests of Nova Scotia, Canada. The native Mi'kmaq people considered the moose and other all-white animals as spiritual beings that should never be harmed. The thought of shooting such a precious animal was simply unimaginable to them. So when a trio of non-native hunters killed the moose in 2013 and posted photos on social media, the Mi'kmaq were grief-stricken, shocked and angry. They also thought that such a senseless act would bring bad luck to those who did it. The remorseful hunters returned the moose's hide so the tribe could perform a four-day ceremony to honour the animal. Thanks to White Moose, animal advocates are pushing for new laws to protect other wild albino animals from harm.

POLAR WILDLIFE WINS

Global warming is a global warning, but there are signs of hope for polar regions:

- A huge colony of 1.5 million Adélie penguins was discovered near Antarctica in 2018, a welcome boost to the world's declining penguin population.

- The Antarctic Treaty of 1961 kick-started a series of agreements to protect the wildlife of this special continent. There are also strict measures in place to prevent pollution in the world's most pristine wilderness.

- As their native habitat vanishes, polar bears are edging ever closer to human settlements in search of food. This puts both the bears and the people in grave danger. Karelian bear dogs are now being trained to bark and scare the bears away, so Arctic inhabitants of both species stay safe.

- A relic of the last Ice Age, the shaggy-haired musk ox has lived in the Arctic for thousands of years. At one point, there were only 5,000 left but now there are over 80,000. Wildlife conservation works!

- Edinburgh Zoo in Scotland has been famous for its penguins since 1913. Three king penguins arrived that year and were the first ever to breed outside the South Atlantic. Today, the zoo is internationally renowned for its penguin conservation programme.

- The town of Churchill in Manitoba, Canada, is famous for its "polar bear jail". Any bear that insists on visiting the town uninvited is isolated in this building before being escorted to a safer spot. In the past, bears that wandered too close were shot, so relocating them is a much better option.

- Large vessels pose a threat to wildlife, so many new polar-class ships are designed to be quieter and "greener", with fewer carbon emissions. Many tour operators now give their passengers opportunities to get involved with conservation projects too.

- Snow petrels spit to feed their young and persuade predators to back off. Now layers of ancient snow petrel spit are helping scientists in Antarctica predict how the birds will respond to climate change. Most Antarctic seabirds head north during the winter, but snow petrels stay put even when the ocean is covered in ice. *Brrr!*

OTHER AMAZING POLAR ANIMALS

A bar-tailed godwit known as **E7** holds the world record for the longest non-stop flight, a journey of 11,500 kilometres (7,200 miles). The bird completed her 2007 marathon flight from Alaska to New Zealand in eight days straight, without stopping once to eat, drink or sleep.

During a bad Arctic storm in 1950, an exhausted snowy owl appeared out of nowhere and fell to the deck of HMS *Eros*. The captain named him **EROS** and later presented him to London Zoo. He lived there for more than forty years and fathered nearly sixty chicks.

At the Point Defiance Zoo in Washington State, USA, romance blossomed between musk oxen **HUDSON AND CHARLOTTE** in 2020. Suspecting a baby might be on the way, keepers confirmed Charlotte's pregnancy in a rather ingenious way – they mixed edible glitter into her food so they could tell which piles of poo were hers for testing.

An orphaned polar bear named **KNUT** (pronounced *Kah-noot*), born at Berlin Zoo in 2006, inspired a craze dubbed "Knutmania". Billed as "the world's most famous polar bear", he was featured on the cover of *Vanity Fair*

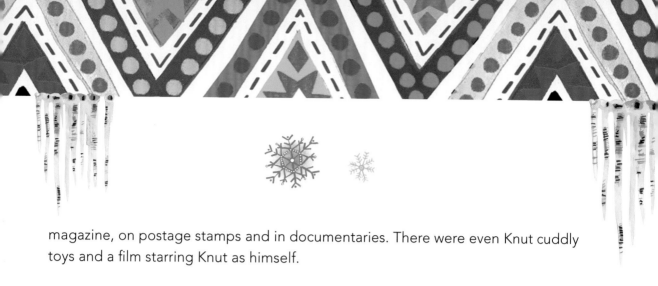

magazine, on postage stamps and in documentaries. There were even Knut cuddly toys and a film starring Knut as himself.

When two musk oxen at Finland's Ranua Zoo, **MAX AND BODIL**, had their baby **OUNA** in 2016, it was the first time a musk ox calf had been born in the region since the last Ice Age. That was nearly 12,000 years ago!

Chinstrap penguins **ROY AND SILO** lived at Central Park Zoo in New York City, USA. After they attempted to hatch a rock in 1999, keepers gave them an egg to nurture as their own. Similarly, gentoo penguins **MAGIC AND SPHEN** adopted a chick after a trial run with a fake egg at the Sydney Sea Life Aquarium in Australia.

SIR NILS OLAV, a king penguin at Edinburgh Zoo, is the only penguin with a knighthood and military rank. Soldiers of lower rank in the Norwegian King's Guard are required to salute him!

The Isle of Skye in Scotland has two resident sea eagles, **VICTOR AND ORLA**, who have raised chicks there for years. The birds are native to the Arctic, where they were hunted nearly to extinction in the early twentieth century. There's now a thriving population once again.

ASIA AND THE PACIFIC

Animals being killed for their body parts – such as rhino horns, tiger bones and pangolin scales – is a big reason why many species are now in serious trouble. A growing number of conservationists say that traditional Chinese medicine is contributing to the deadly demand for endangered wildlife.

Traditional Chinese medicine (TCM) is the world's oldest form of healthcare, dating back thousands of years. This ancient practice features all sorts of therapies and treatments, such as herbal remedies, massage and acupuncture. Although people all across Asia also rely on science-based medicine, TCM remains very popular and has spread to over 180 countries worldwide.

Wild animal parts are found in many TCM products, despite little evidence to back their health claims. Fortunately, attitudes throughout Asia are changing towards TCM, especially among the younger generation.

Today, more and more TCM practitioners refuse to prescribe medicines that contain ingredients from endangered animals. Chinese health insurance no longer pays for such products either. Wildlife conservation is becoming better understood and there's a new global treaty that protects animals from being harmed for traditional medicine. China and some other Asian countries have banned the import of ivory too.

In 2020, China banned the sale of wildlife for meat, added more protections for pangolins and removed pangolin scales from a list of approved TCM ingredients. While the country hasn't ended the illegal hunting of endangered species, it's definitely a step in the right direction.

RUSSIA

MONGOLIA

PAKISTAN

JAPAN

NEPAL

CHINA

PACIFIC
OCEAN

INDIA

LAOS

THAILAND

VIETNAM

SRI LANKA

MALAYSIA

BORNEO

INDIAN
OCEAN

BOTOK BACTRIAN CAMEL

Botok was the star of *The Story of the Weeping Camel*, a film featuring a family of nomadic shepherds in Mongolia's Gobi Desert. The shepherds struggled to save the life of the rare white Bactrian camel calf after his mother rejected him. The helpless baby wouldn't survive without his mother's care and milk, so the desperate herders finally resorted to an ancient ritual. A violinist came and played a mystical song while the herders stroked the mother camel and whispered encouragement. Miraculously, the ritual worked – the mother started to nuzzle Botok and eventually allowed him to feed. The film gives a magical insight into the life of the Mongolian herders and their animals. A very special documentary, it was nominated for Best Foreign Film at the 2004 Academy Awards. If only Botok could have been there to strut down the red carpet!

COCONUT SNOW LEOPARD

Coconut lives at Sacramento Zoo in California, USA, where he was born in 2018 with a condition known as "swimmer's syndrome". The youngster's hind limbs splayed out behind him and he was unable to put any weight on them. Experts rushed to the cub's aid, but his mum wasn't too keen at first about anyone getting near her precious baby. The vets eventually gained her trust and designed a physical therapy programme that included tiny slings and harnesses to help Coconut stand and walk and strengthen his muscles. By his first birthday, the curious and playful cub was running and pouncing and was as lively as a young leopard should be. Coconut's against-all-odds saga provided a rare opportunity for zoo visitors to learn more about Asia's mysterious and rarely seen "ghost cats".

KINGUT TAPIR

Kingut was born in captivity in Indonesia and was moved to England when he was a teenager. For nearly three decades, he participated in a breeding programme for endangered species operated by the Aspinall Foundation. Kingut later retired to a 250-hectare (600-acre) wildlife sanctuary to live with four younger Malayan tapirs. Tapirs tend to be solitary creatures who prefer having their own space, but Kingut is unique – he gets jealous if the other tapirs get more attention and used to chase his caregivers around just for fun. In 2019, the plump black-and-white tapir celebrated an important birthday with a scrummy cake made from bananas, apples and carrots, all his favourite treats. At forty-one, Kingut was recognized as the oldest of his kind by Guinness World Records.

LING-LING AND HSING-HSING GIANT PANDAS

When US President Richard Nixon visited Asia in 1972, the Chinese leader gave him a very special gift – a pair of giant pandas. The bears were intended to be living symbols of peace and friendship between the two countries. Female Ling-Ling and male Hsing-Hsing became overnight celebrities and people around the globe followed their long journey to Washington, DC. After the couple was welcomed to America by the president's wife, they were whisked away to the National Zoo in the capital under an escort of armed guards. Ling-Ling and Hsing-Hsing drew 20,000 visitors on their first day on display and almost doubled the number of visitors to the zoo. They lived at the zoo all their lives and taught researchers an enormous amount about pandas.

MACHLI BENGAL TIGER

Machli lived in a national park in northern India, where she reigned as queen of the jungle and earned a reputation for being utterly fearless. She had to defend her territory and young cubs again and again from much larger male tigers, and once she even took on and killed a gigantic crocodile. She did all these things on camera too, appearing in magazines and on television programmes all around the world. Machli passed away in her sleep in 2016 when she was about 19 years old, an impressive age for a female tiger. The heartbroken local people insisted on honouring her with a traditional Hindu funeral. Wrapped in white linen and adorned with flower garlands, her body was cremated as forest rangers respectfully stood to attention.

MARTHA SAOLA

A saola is a creature so rare and elusive that they're known as the "Asian unicorn". In 1996, a young female was captured in Laos. Named Martha, she looked like a miniature antelope and was one of the most astonishing discoveries of the twentieth century – the first living saola that scientists had ever seen. She was beautiful and very shy, but soon grew tame enough to eat out of a researcher's hand and even allowed herself to be gently stroked. Sadly, Martha survived only a few weeks in captivity, and to this day no biologist has ever seen a saola living in the wild. Conservationists now hope to find a pair of saolas and start a captive breeding programme in Vietnam. More than two decades after her death, their dream is to give Martha's story a much happier ending.

PRINCESS ORANGUTAN

Orangutans are considered one of the smartest primates and Princess was especially brainy. After poachers killed her mum in the 1970s, she was sold as an exotic pet but later rescued and returned to the wild in Borneo. She drove local researchers mad, sometimes helping herself to their dugout canoe so she could paddle up and down the river. One time, a visiting scientist struggled to open the door to his hut. The lock had been designed to keep the clever apes out, but Princess plucked the key from his hand, opened the door and bolted it behind her. Then she ate an entire bowl of fruit that had been left as his welcome gift! What Princess is best known for, however, is mastering over 30 words in sign language, a remarkable feat for an animal living outside captivity.

WISDOM ALBATROSS

Wisdom is the world's oldest known wild bird and she's flown millions of miles over the course of her long life. Albatrosses are large birds that spend the majority of their lives at sea, only returning to their nesting sites on land to breed. They mate for life and typically lay a single egg every other year or so. Yet Wisdom and her mate, Akeakamai, have returned to the same site in Midway Atoll in the Pacific Ocean every season for many years, laying an egg each time. Wisdom has raised more than 35 chicks and in 2019 became a mother once again at the age of 68. Albatrosses are no longer hunted for their feathers, but seas polluted with oil, microplastics and other rubbish continue to threaten the species.

ASIAN WILDLIFE WINS

Conservationists throughout Asia are making great strides in their quest to save threatened species:

- Conservation dogs in India are being trained to sniff out tiger skins, ivory tusks and the bones of endangered birds. They can also locate injured wildlife, which helps rangers track down and arrest poachers more quickly.

- The Giant Panda Breeding Research Base in Chengdu, China, is home to over a hundred giant pandas. Giant pandas rarely breed in captivity, but at Chengdu there has been greater success. The keepers do everything they can to give the pandas a natural life, including wearing black-and-white costumes so the pandas won't get too used to humans!

- A new Giant Panda Nature Reserve in China will connect 67 protected giant panda territories, giving the bears room to roam freely and find mates.

- The Gobi Bear Project in Mongolia helps protect the bears by setting up feeding stations in the Gobi Desert and guarding them with rangers on motorbikes.

- Four baby Javan rhinos – one of the world's rarest species – were born in 2020 in a national park in Indonesia, bringing the total population up to 72. The park is the only place these rhinos can be found in the wild.

ENDANGERED

VULNERABLE

* A pango-cam is a lightweight, waterproof camera that can be attached to the back of a pangolin. These animals are difficult to observe in the wild, so the pango-cam helps researchers learn more about them by giving them a unique pangolin's-eye view.

* Conservationists created a special school for orangutans on the island of Borneo to teach orphaned apes how to eat, live and sleep in trees – all key survival skills their mums would have taught them.

* Ten baby Siamese crocodiles were spotted in the wild in Cambodia in early 2020, a sign that breeding programmes are working. Locals are helping too by patrolling the forest alongside rangers to stop poachers.

* The Skywalker hoolock gibbon was named by scientists who were big fans of the Star Wars films. They thought "sky walker" was an accurate description of the apes' movement high in the forest canopy. Fun names are also a clever way to draw people's attention to at-risk species.

* There are fewer than 400 Sumatran tigers left in the wild due to poaching and habitat loss. New laws are putting traffickers behind bars and more rangers are being hired to protect tigers.

OTHER AMAZING ASIAN ANIMALS

ALBA is the world's only known albino orangutan. She was released into the wild in 2018 in Borneo and conservationists spotted her swinging joyfully through the trees the following year.

CHARLIE is a Komodo dragon who gave birth to three hatchlings – **ONYX, JASPER** and **FLINT** – in 2019, without any help from a male partner. (Yes, it's possible with some species!) The lizard family lives at Chattanooga Zoo in Tennessee, USA.

A rare **CHINESE PANGOLIN** was born in captivity for the first time in 2020 at a sanctuary in Vietnam. The team at Save Vietnam's Wildlife were taken by surprise when they spotted the little guy trotting along behind his mother. They now feel very optimistic about future breeding programmes.

CLARA was an Indian rhinoceros who caused a sensation during her 17-year grand tour of Europe in the mid-eighteenth century. Such a creature hadn't been seen in Europe since 1579 and people treated her like a rhino rock star everywhere she went.

The Sumatran rhinoceros went extinct in Malaysia in late 2019 when the country's last female rhino, **IMAN**, died of cancer. **TAM**, Malaysia's last male rhino, died earlier that spring. The species is now down to about 80 individuals, all living in Indonesia.

LINGHAN was in pretty rough shape and nearly blind when he was found in 2019 in a remote region of Tibet. Chinese vets made history by performing cataract surgery on the snow leopard, successfully restoring his vision.

NING NONG saved the life of a British girl when a tsunami hit Thailand in 2004. Amber Mason was riding on the elephant's back when Ning Nong sensed that something was wrong, well before anyone else did. She scurried to higher ground and saved Amber from being drowned.

Two chicks from the world's rarest owl species have survived to become fledglings for the first time in 10 years. There are fewer than 50 **NORFOLK ISLAND MOREPORK OWLS** left on a remote island in the Pacific Ocean. Hopefully the tiny pair, born in 2020, will help save their species.

ZHANG XIANG was the first captive-bred female panda to be released into a protected wilderness area, in 2013. She was still alive and well years later, giving conservationists great cause for celebration.

AUSTRALIA AND NEW ZEALAND

Surrounded by ocean, the wildlife of the island countries of Australia and New Zealand has evolved separately from that of their nearest neighbours and from each other. Animals such as the koala, kea and quokka are found nowhere else.

When Europeans arrived in the eighteenth century, they brought rats, livestock and diseases with them that pushed some native species to the brink of extinction. Nowadays, climate change caused by humans also poses a danger to Australian wildlife.

The first mammal to die out as a direct result of climate change was the Bramble Cay melomys. The little rodents lived in only one place on earth, a sand island off the northern coast of Australia. A local fisherman was the last person to see one alive in the wild in 2009. Ten years later, this species was officially declared gone for ever.

Climate change has also sparked terrible natural disasters throughout the region. The 2019 bushfires in Australia were particularly bad due to drought, scorching temperatures and strong winds caused by global warming. It's estimated that over three billion animals died or were forced from their habitats.

Sad facts like this are tough to think about. Yet it's important to remember that Australia is a gigantic place and the bushfires burned only a fraction of it. The impact on wildlife was devastating, but many animals did survive, and there are now positive signs that ecosystems are bouncing back and landscapes are recovering.

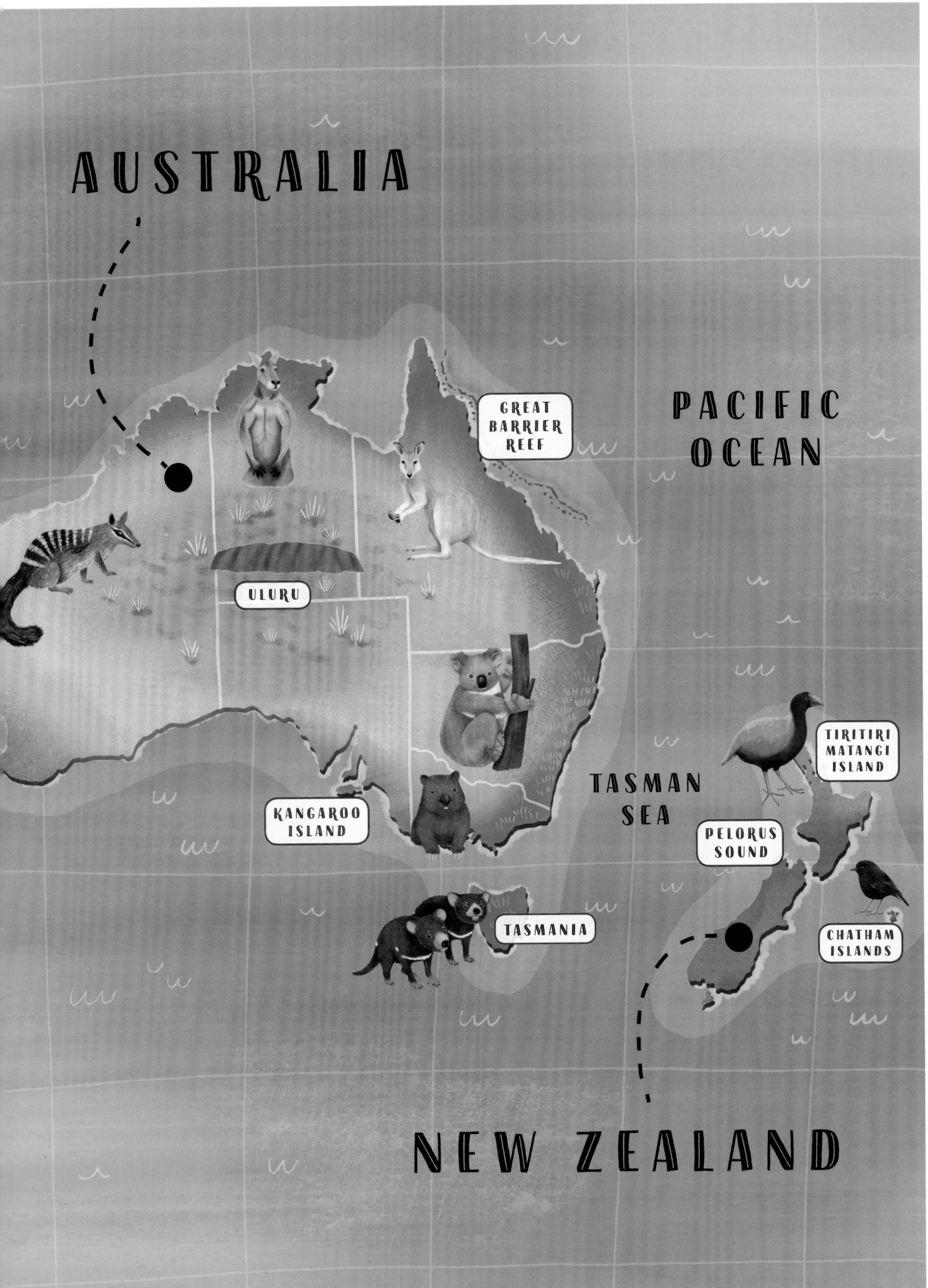

AUSTRALIA

PACIFIC OCEAN

GREAT
BARRIER
REEF

ULURU

KANGAROO
ISLAND

TASMAN
SEA

TIRITIRI
MATANGI
ISLAND

PELORUS
SOUND

CHATHAM
ISLANDS

TASMANIA

NEW ZEALAND

ANWEN KOALA

Anwen was one of the first koalas treated at the Port Macquarie Koala Hospital after the bushfires of 2019. Instead of fleeing the flames, koalas instinctively climbed up trees to escape danger, so the youngster was badly burned. Volunteers spent days giving her fluids and putting ointment on her injuries. As Anwen recovered, she began to look forward to the daily delivery of fresh eucalyptus leaves. She also found a perch the staff dubbed "Anwen's spot", where she could sit and prop up her sore paws. Photos of the fuzzy marsupial on the hospital's online adoption page introduced her to thousands of well-wishers who followed her progress. Anwen was eventually returned to the wild and became a symbol of hope for a nation of traumatized animal lovers.

APPLE WALLABY

Apple hopped into the lobby of the Thala Beach eco-resort one day and quickly became a regular and popular visitor. She was a natural crowd-pleaser, greeting guests upon arrival, munching on carrots and posing for selfies. Sometimes she even rested a paw on a lucky visitor's knee, her marsupial version of a friendly handshake. Frequently mistaken for a young kangaroo, Apple was actually a wild wallaby and probably the only one with her own social media hashtag, #AppletheWallaby. Guests loved to share their favourite holiday photos of Apple and she was also featured in numerous magazines, newspapers and YouTube videos. She passed away in late 2016, leaving behind a little joey called Coco, who was well looked after until he was able to be returned to the wild.

DASH AND VIOLET TASMANIAN DEVILS

Two tiny Tasmanian devils were found in 2018, helpless and alone with no mother in sight. Named Dash and Violet after characters in the animated film *The Incredibles*, the twins soon became known as the "incre-devils". They now live at the Australian Reptile Park, where they are a key part of a captive breeding programme. Dash and Violet are social media stars, with millions of fans watching them grow up. Celebrations for the mischievous pair's first birthday included treats hidden in boxes, which they ripped apart in typical toddler fashion, and a cake made of finely chopped meat. The twins are teaching people that members of their species are not "devils" at all – they're total sweethearts, although they have been known to make some spine-chilling sounds!

GREG TAKAHE

Takahes are flightless birds that for decades were believed to be extinct. Tiritiri Matangi in New Zealand is one of the few places where they can be found in the wild and Greg was one of the island's best-known birds. He arrived there in 1994 as a youngster and quickly got busy boosting the takahe population, fathering many chicks over the years. He had no fear of humans and came to associate them with food – if you weren't careful, he'd stalk off with your lunch! He was so popular that a children's book was written about him, *Greg the Naughty Takahe*. After he died in 2012, Greg's admirers held a ceremony to celebrate his life and set up a conservation fund in his memory. Today, the takahe population is still quite small but growing, with more than 400 birds.

OLD BLUE BLACK ROBIN

Old Blue was a black robin (aka Chatham Island robin), a species found only in New Zealand. At one time there were just five birds left and Old Blue was the only adult female. It seemed like a hopeless situation, but one biologist came up with a radical plan. Each time Old Blue laid eggs, he put them in "foster nests" to be hatched by other birds, prompting her to lay more. It worked so well that all 250 black robins alive today are descendants of Old Blue. She was honoured on a postage stamp and a coin, inspired a children's book and has a plaque dedicated to her at the Chatham Islands Airport. She's also the only bird in history whose death was formally announced at a government's parliament. And rightly so, as Old Blue saved her entire species from becoming extinct.

PATRICK WOMBAT

Patrick came to the Ballarat Wildlife Park in 1987 and soon endeared himself to everyone with his gentle nature and buck-toothed grin. Voted one of the world's best city mascots by CNN Travel, Patrick appeared in YouTube videos and on the TV programme *Totally Wild*. He loved cuddles and zooming around the park in his personalized blue wheelbarrow, and he met a number of famous people – including royalty. Patrick had over 55,000 Facebook fans but never found a special female, not even after his keepers signed him up for an online dating service. In 2017, Patrick celebrated his thirty-first birthday with hundreds of friends. He passed away a short time later, the oldest known bare-nosed wombat in captivity.

ROGER KANGAROO

A kind man rescued Roger from his mum's pouch after she was killed in a road accident. Named after the animated film star Roger Rabbit, the young joey grew to a mammoth size – more than two metres tall and 99 kilograms (six feet seven inches and 196 pounds) – with a buff physique that set him apart from other male 'roos. He appeared in the BBC documentary *Kangaroo Dundee*, but true fame came after a 2015 video went viral. It showed him crushing a metal bucket with his bare paws! This incredible feat of strength made "Ripped Roger" an internet sensation. The massive marsupial died in 2018 when he was 12 years old. The Kangaroo Sanctuary that was created especially for Roger now keeps his memory alive with its 'roo rehab and conservation programmes.

WHISKEY NUMBAT

Whiskey was born at Perth Zoo in 2015 and played a key role in the zoo's breeding programme, fathering many numbats that were later released into the wild. Numbats are pint-sized marsupials with bottle-brush tails that were at risk of extinction just a few decades ago. Their biggest threats are habitat loss and foxes, which Europeans introduced in the 1800s. Today there are still fewer than a thousand in Western Australia but things are improving, especially after the government funded numbat conservation in 2018 – a gift timed to celebrate the birth of Prince Louis, the newest member of the British royal family. Now enjoying a well-deserved retirement, Whiskey is a favourite with visiting schoolchildren and serves as an excellent ambassador for his species.

AUSTRALIAN AND NEW ZEALAND WILDLIFE WINS

The 2019 bushfires dealt a terrible blow to Australian wildlife, but there are still many positive things to report:

🐾 Bandicoots now have their own predator-free island, part of a programme to boost their declining numbers. Fifty-five of the miniscule marsupials were released in 2019 on French Island, located off the southeast coast of Australia.

🐾 Australians can buy chocolate bilbies for Easter instead of chocolate bunnies. It's a conservation campaign to raise awareness of the tiny, big-eared creatures and their endangered status.

🐾 Drones are high-tech tools used to help rescue Australian wildlife. The drones can cover lots of territory in a short time, ideal for locating bushfire survivors and doing visual health checks.

🐾 In New Zealand, drones are also helping kakapos, the world's largest species of parrot, by helping scientists track the dwindling population and spot problems as soon as they arise.

🐾 The conservation group Kiwis for Kiwi collects kiwi eggs and hatchlings and rears them in safe locations until they are old enough to survive on their own.

🐾 After the koala population dropped by two-thirds in 20 years, conservationists requested an emergency "endangered" listing for koalas to give them additional protections.

🐾 Maremma dogs now work as "bodyguards" for bandicoots, which have been virtually wiped out in Australia by predators.

🐾 A new national park in New South Wales was created solely to provide a protected habitat for at least 27 endangered species, including the grey grasswren, a small bird native to the area.

🐾 Knitters made tiny sweaters for oil-soaked penguins after a 2001 spill on Australia's Phillip Island. The sweaters prevented the birds from grooming themselves and swallowing the harmful oil.

🐾 The critically endangered smoky mouse was initially thought extinct after the bushfires of 2019, but they've since been spotted alive on camera at seven sites in New South Wales, Australia.

🐾 After the 2019 bushfires wiped out huge areas of habitat, wildlife rangers in Australia dumped bushels of carrots and sweet potatoes from planes to feed wallabies and other hungry animals.

🐾 Wombats, which look like giant guinea pigs and are one of the world's most endangered species, are now legally protected in every state in Australia.

OTHER AMAZING AUSTRALIAN ANIMALS

AJAX is the world's only conservation dog who specializes in kea. He and his handler roam New Zealand's South Island in search of nests so the birds can be tagged and monitored.

A conservation dog called **BEAR** is trained to sniff out koala scat and fur. Wearing socks to protect his paws, he is sent into burnt-out areas to search for sick and injured animals. He found over a hundred koalas after the 2019 Australian bushfires!

The last known Tasmanian tiger, **BENJAMIN**, died at a zoo in 1936. Each year on 7 September, the anniversary of his death, Australia observes National Threatened Species Day in his memory.

DAVEY is a quokka who is said to have psychic powers. He accurately predicted the outcomes of various elections and major sporting events based on which food bowl he opted to eat from first.

MR WOO was a rare albino wallaby adopted by a British rescue centre in 2004. He became a celebrity, appearing on television programmes such as *Blue Peter*.

A dog called **REX** found a young joey in a mother kangaroo's pouch after she'd been killed on a road. Named **REX JUNIOR** after his saviour, the joey lived at a sanctuary until he was old enough to return to the wild.

SAM was a badly burned koala who gained fame when photos of her went viral in 2009. The images showed her guzzling from a water bottle held by a firefighter during the Black Saturday bushfires, one of Australia's worst natural disasters. Sam's survival story inspired many people to support and donate to the Australian Koala Foundation.

A herd of **WILD WALLABIES** live on the Isle of Man in the UK. It's thought that a group of the bouncy marsupials made a bid for freedom from a local wildlife park back in the 1960s. Now the island has around 150 of them, the largest wallaby population in the northern hemisphere.

WANDI mysteriously appeared out of nowhere in a backyard in Australia in 2019. His DNA revealed that he was a very rare thing – a pure-bred Australian alpine dingo. Judging by the scratches on his back, experts believe he was dropped out of the sky by an eagle! He now lives at a sanctuary in Victoria.

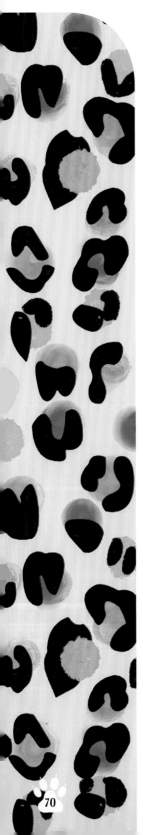

EUROPE

In our ever more crowded world, humans are creating a lot of problems for wildlife. This can especially be seen in many densely populated places in Europe.

The more people there are, the more towns and cities, roads and railways, houses and office buildings. All of which can harm wildlife and destroy their natural habitats.

Wildlife in the countryside is in danger too. More and more land is being ploughed up to grow crops to feed our increasing population, and those crops are often doused with chemicals that are toxic to animals.

It may feel as if we are losing touch with the natural world, but if we look and listen, it's possible to find wildlife even in a sprawling, noisy metropolis. Peregrine falcons, for example, were considered extinct in southern Britain in the 1960s. Now new protections and limits on pesticides have allowed their numbers to bounce back, even in places you might not expect – like the British capital, London!

Today, there are about 30 pairs of peregrine falcons soaring high over London's concrete canyons and brick cliff faces. Two of the best-known falcons are Charlie and Augustus. They live at a very prestigious address, the Houses of Parliament, where they have a fancy nesting box, a nest cam and their very own Facebook page.

It just goes to show that it is indeed possible to peacefully co-exist with the wild animals that share our planet.

ICELAND

SCOTLAND

NORTH
SEA

ENGLAND

NORTH
ATLANTIC

FINLAND

DENMARK

RUSSIA

BLACK SEA

MEDITERRANEAN SEA

CELLIE HEDGEHOG

Cellie was found trapped in a cellar on a cold winter night in 2001. Thin and weak, he was so hungry that he was trying to eat an old shoe. His rescuers rushed him to a woman, Joan, who ran a hedgehog hospital in England. Joan didn't think Cellie would survive but he defied all odds and became her constant companion, scurrying after her wherever she went. He became the star of Joan's public education programme, happy to be stroked and cuddled on visits to schools, libraries and care homes – even a prison once. The friendly hog was a prickly professional, featuring on TV and in newspapers as he helped raise awareness about the dangers hedgehogs face and how people can help them. Cellie may have been little, but he made a big impression on all who met him.

KATRINE SCOTTISH WILDCAT

Katrine was born at the Highland Wildlife Park in Scotland, a sanctuary where wildcats live in large natural enclosures. After she was paired with a male cat in 2019, conservationists used remote cameras to keep an eye on her. Katrine's belly appeared suspiciously large, but weeks went by with no sign of her giving birth. One camera finally captured footage of Katrine moving a kitten into her nest box. The park staff watched hours of film and noticed that Katrine seemed to be moving her kitten around a lot. It soon became clear there was a second kitten … and another … and another. Four kittens for a first-time mum! The staff were amazed – Scottish wildcats usually only have one kitten per litter. There may be as few as 100 wildcats left, so Katrine's already making a big contribution to saving Britain's rarest mammal from extinction.

LEN PRZEWALSKI'S HORSE

Len is the grandson of the last Przewalski's horse born in the wild. "P horses" are the world's only surviving species of wild horse, and large herds of them once roamed the vast plains of Russia and central Asia. Yet by the 1960s, there was no sign of even a single one still living there. Len was born in captivity in Ukraine in 2002 and relocated to Prague Zoo. A bashful stallion with notched ears, Len is pretty laid back but still wild at heart, refusing to let anyone touch him or shut him inside a pen. In 2011, he fathered a filly and went on to sire several other foals. One of his daughters, Querida, was returned to the land of her ancestors and now lives there wild and free amongst others of her own kind, just as Len's grandmother once did.

LINDA EURASIAN LYNX

A hungry cat crept inside Leningrad Zoo in 2008 and followed her nose to an enclosure. She found a yummy meal but also put herself in danger as a Eurasian lynx called Linda slowly approached. Lynxes are big, solitary creatures and Linda could have killed the intruder with one smack of her giant paw. Yet she welcomed the tiny cat and didn't seem to mind sharing her food. The kitty started visiting Linda every day and the zoo eventually adopted her and named her Dusya. The feline friends spend their days hanging out together and playing with their favourite toy, a cardboard box. They're also a big hit on Russian social media and have thousands of devoted followers. As this big-cat-little-cat friendship shows, you never know where you might find a new bestie!

TIN TIN RED SQUIRREL

Tin Tin was only five weeks old when he fell from a rooftop in 2016 and was badly injured. A Danish man brought him inside and allowed his cat Coco to comfort the little squirrel and purr him to sleep. Tin Tin recovered with lots of TLC and was soon riding around in his rescuer's pocket. While it's usually illegal to keep squirrels as pets in Denmark, an exception was made for Tin Tin due to his obvious bond with his human. After Coco passed away, the man's other cat, Tiger, became the squirrel's protector, following by his little friend's side when Tin Tin was on his leash for walks. Tin Tin loves solving puzzles, has a knack for sensing when someone feels down and brings smiles to the faces of 134,000 Instagram fans each day. How many squirrels can say that?

TÓTI PUFFIN

The renowned Sæheimar Aquarium in Iceland has cared for a number of injured puffins over the years, but Tóti was perhaps the most memorable. The day he was rescued, a local football player called Tóti scored a winning goal and the puffin was named in his honour. People loved to give Tóti puffin-sized football shirts and see him wearing them in photos posted on social media. With his cheerful striped beak and waddling walk, adorable Tóti could be counted on to charm all the aquarium's visitors. Many people wrote reviews saying the celebrity bird was the highlight of their trip. After Tóti passed away in 2018, the aquarium staff posted an official announcement that said, "Tóti was a small puffin with a large heart who brought joy to everyone who met him."

VEETI EUROPEAN MINK

Veeti is described by his keepers as "goofy", known for running about his enclosure like a mad fool and often taking a tumble because he's too busy to watch where he's going. He also has a reputation for startling onlookers by falling out of trees, sometimes back first, then springing to his feet and racing off again. Veeti lives at the Ranua Wildlife Park, the northernmost zoo in Finland, a country where European minks were once very common. Sadly, they are now extinct in the wild in Finland and are considered critically endangered elsewhere in Europe. Mischievous Veeti plays an important role in the European Endangered Species Programme, which aims to breed the water-loving animals and reintroduce them in protected areas throughout the Baltic Sea region.

WHISKY BARN OWL

Whisky had been abused and was missing her beak when she arrived at the Blue Highlands bird sanctuary in northern Scotland. She had to be fed tiny bites of food until a prosthetic beak was created for her. Her beak grew back over time and Whisky began helping to teach people about her unique species – like the fact that a single barn owl can kill a thousand mice a year! Thanks to their animal-catching skills, barn owls have been helping keep humans safe for centuries by preventing the spread of vermin and disease. Despite all the trauma of her early life, Whisky prefers to stick close to her caregivers and enjoys interacting with visitors, even allowing them to stroke and hold her. If she's feeling especially joyful, she'll even do a little dance for them!

EUROPEAN WILDLIFE WINS

Just as Britain's urban peregrine falcons have staged a comeback, so too have many other species throughout Europe:

- 🐾 The Land of the Leopard National Park, a wildlife sanctuary in Russia, has helped endangered Amur leopards claw their way back from near extinction.

- 🐾 Beavers became extinct in Britain over 400 years ago, but it is hoped that reintroducing them may prevent flooding. Their dam-building skills make them excellent eco-engineers!

- 🐾 Hedgehog crossing signs in Britain alert motorists to watch out for the prickly critters on roads. This is important because the number of hedgehogs has declined ninety-five per cent since the 1950s.

- 🐾 In Spain, a major conservation plan was put in place to help Iberian lynxes when their numbers fell below one hundred in the wild. It worked! Iberian lynxes have moved from Critically Endangered to Endangered on the IUCN Red List.

- 🐾 The first Przewalski's horse in modern times was born with the help of artificial insemination in 2013, an exciting breakthrough for the species.

- Red kites are a conservation success story in the UK. Thirty years after 13 of these birds of prey were flown in from Spain, there are now 1,800 breeding pairs across the country.

- Prince Charles is such a fan of red squirrels that he gives them names and allows them inside his Scottish home. He hopes to establish a predator-free sanctuary for red squirrels someday.

- Scottish wildcats are now protected under British law and plans are in the works to create a captive population that will eventually be released into the wild.

- More and more countries in Europe have banned wild animals in circuses, including Austria, England, the Netherlands, Scotland and Slovakia.

- The world's first wildlife crossing was built in France in the 1950s. There are now thousands of "green bridges" and tunnels across the world, enabling animals to cross roads and railways safely.

- Wolves are being reintroduced to European countries where they have died out, and sheepdogs are helping protect livestock from them. Protecting livestock protects the wolves from angry farmers too!

ENDANGERED

VULNERABLE

EXTINCT

OTHER AMAZING EUROPEAN ANIMALS

Wolf parents **AUGUST** and **NOELLA** produced four cubs in 2020. The youngsters were the first wild wolf cubs to be born in Belgium in more than 150 years.

Feisty **EJ** was a female osprey who returned each year to a reserve in the Scottish Highlands. She raised 23 chicks but gained even greater fame for her dramatic squabbles with other birds.

GB07 was a white stork mum who hatched three chicks on a castle estate in West Sussex, England, in 2020. They were the first stork chicks born in the wild in the UK for over 600 years.

Golden eagle **GOLDIE** lived at London Zoo in the 1960s. He made headlines when he escaped and spent two weeks playing tag with his keepers. After Goldie was finally caught, zoo attendance nearly doubled.

When land is being developed, hedgehogs often find themselves in great danger. Welsh springer spaniel **HENRY** helps sniff out the hedgehogs so they can be relocated to safe and snug new homes.

MACCA, a fox terrier from New Zealand, was hired in 2018 to help protect wildlife on Scotland's Orkney Islands. He's a conservation detection dog trained to find

ENDANGERED

VULNERABLE

EXTINCT

stoats, an invasive species that pose a threat to Orkney's wildlife.

Two female Iberian lynxes, **OLAVIDE** and **OFELIA**, were released in Spain in 2019. Born in captivity in Portugal, they were relocated to Spain to help improve the species' genetic diversity.

A brown bear nicknamed **PAPILLON** escaped from an enclosure in northern Italy in 2020, scaling three electrified fences and a four-metre-high barrier. He's done it not once but twice! One conservationist urged authorities not to kill the fugitive, saying, "He's guilty only of loving freedom, like all of us."

TURBULENT KNIGHT is a European bison born in the Czech Republic and moved to the Netherlands in 2020. The young bull was named by students in Austria.

VALI, a grizzly bear at Budapest Zoo, saved a crow from drowning when she rescued it from her enclosure's pool in 2014. The dramatic rescue was widely shared on social media.

WOJTEK was a brown bear adopted by Polish soldiers during the Second World War. He helped them win a key battle by lugging heavy boxes of ammunition to the front lines and went on to spend a peaceful retirement at Edinburgh Zoo in Scotland.

NORTH AND CENTRAL AMERICA

Many Native Americans believe that humans were created to serve as caretakers of the earth. But Mother Earth can be complicated, and it is not always easy to work out how best to look after it.

The world's first national park was Yellowstone in North America, established in 1872. Just over a century later, Yellowstone's ecosystem was badly out of balance, with far too many prey animals and not enough predators. A decision was made to restore the park's natural equilibrium to the way it used to be, before Europeans came and killed off all the wolves who once roamed the area.

Not everyone was sure about it, but bringing wolves back to Yellowstone turned out to be a conservation success story. In addition to the wolves, an astonishing number of other animals benefitted, including beavers, bald eagles and bears. The park's flora and fauna flourished in ways that no one had ever dreamed possible.

Even so, the work of conservationists is never done. There is always a place where human interests come into conflict with animals' needs. When the US government passed laws that made it easier for companies to explore for oil and gas in some of America's most beloved national parks, there was a major international outcry. The compromise was a new 2020 law that guaranteed money from oil and gas drilling would be used to support nature and wildlife in national parks – which will benefit humans too!

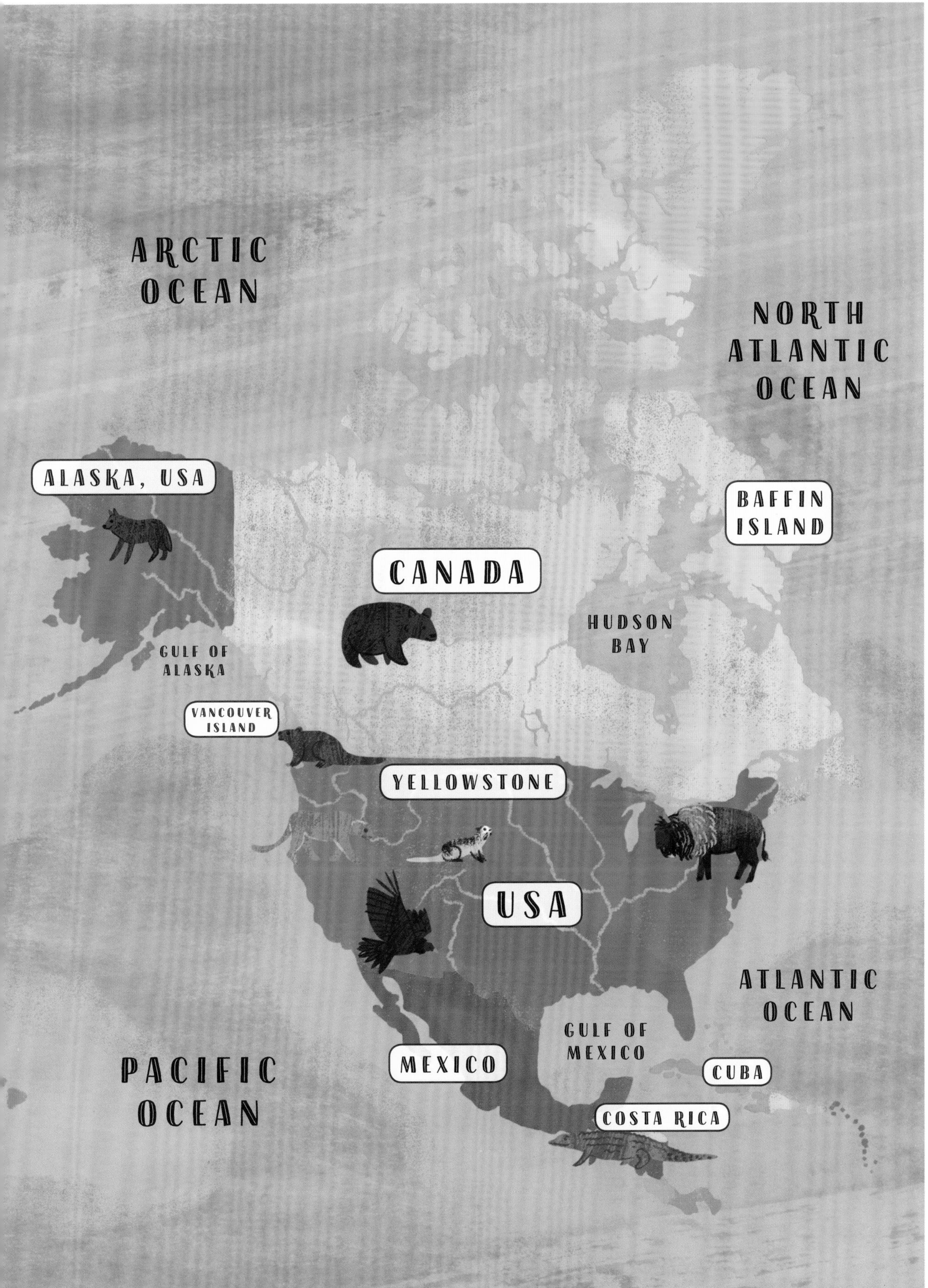

ARCTIC
OCEAN

NORTH
ATLANTIC
OCEAN

ALASKA, USA

BAFFIN
ISLAND

CANADA

HUDSON
BAY

GULF OF
ALASKA

VANCOUVER
ISLAND

YELLOWSTONE

USA

ATLANTIC
OCEAN

PACIFIC
OCEAN

GULF OF
MEXICO

MEXICO

CUBA

COSTA RICA

BLACK DIAMOND AMERICAN BISON

Black Diamond was said to be the inspiration for one of America's best-known coins, the Five Cent Indian Head, better known as the Buffalo Nickel. The popular coin, introduced in 1913, featured a Native American man on the front and a bison on the back. The coin was designed to showcase the beauty of the American West, so it was an honour for Black Diamond to be selected as its model, despite the fact that he lived far away in a big city on the East Coast! Buffalo nickels are now collectors' items and some people believe they bring good luck. American bison today could use some of that luck – while no longer endangered, the species is considered "ecologically extinct" in the wild. Black Diamond's legacy lives on in prized coin collections all around the world.

NATE CONDOR

Everyone feared the worst when Nate the California condor went missing in 2014. As it turned out, the young bird was just stretching his wings like a rebellious teenager and having a little adventure. Make that a big adventure – Nate had embarked on a nine-day, 1,030-kilometre (640-mile) flight from the Grand Canyon to Colorado, USA, and back again. Nicknamed Nate because of his wing tag number, N8, the rare captive-born condor was released into the wild earlier the same year. Local residents scanned the skies and followed his epic journey. His giant wingspan allowed him to soar for miles without ever flapping his wings and he took his time getting back to Arizona, USA. Scientists immediately replaced Nate's tracking device with a new one, not that they needed to. Nate hasn't strayed far from home since!

P-22 MOUNTAIN LION

The life of P-22 sounds like a classic Hollywood rags-to-riches tale – a difficult start and a sudden rise to stardom, followed by international fame. He lives in Griffith Park in Los Angeles, USA, where the famous Hollywood sign can be seen from the observatory. Yet this rarely seen feline and his relatives are in danger of becoming extinct if they can't safely cross Los Angeles' busy freeways and find mates outside their own family. Luckily, there's cause for hope in the form of a much-needed wildlife crossing over a dangerous 10-lane-wide freeway. If P-22's fame can help get the crossing built, the future for southern California's mountain lions will definitely be a lot brighter. That's even better than an Oscar for the feline known as "the Brad Pitt of mountain lions"!

POCHO CROCODILE

Pocho is famous thanks to his longtime friendship with a Costa Rican fisherman named Gilberto "Chito" Shedden. Chito found the half-starved crocodile close to death in 1989, shot through one eye and alone and helpless. Chito took the five-metre-long (15-feet-long) crocodile home and slowly nursed him back to health. As he saw it, Pocho needed love to regain his will to live. After Pocho recovered, he refused to return to the wild and the pair became best buddies. For more than 20 years, Chito and Pocho put on a weekly show to demonstrate their unusual bond and raise awareness about the cruel treatment often inflicted on wildlife. Pocho died in 2011 and hundreds of mourners attended his funeral. He is considered a national treasure in Costa Rica.

ROMEO WOLF

One winter night in 2003, a black wolf appeared near a man's home in Alaska, USA, and his dog ran out to meet it. To his surprise, they started playing with each other. The wolf soon became a regular sight around the area, often fetching balls thrown for him by hikers and skiers. Newspapers published stories about Romeo, the lone wolf who captured the hearts of an entire town. Perhaps it was a friendly wolf like Romeo who first dared to befriend humans around their fires thousands of years ago, leading to the dogs who are our best friends today? Romeo lived to be more than eight years old, more than twice as old as the average wolf in the wild. He inspired a book, *A Wolf Called Romeo*, and the townspeople of Nugget Falls put up a plaque to honour his memory.

SALLY AND PEPSI MARMOTS

Sally and Pepsi lived at a wildlife sanctuary in Canada, where they surprised everyone by becoming the proud parents of three pups in 2019. The largest members of the squirrel family, Vancouver Island marmots had come close to extinction and today there are only about 200 living in the wild. Playing the marmot dating game took a bit of luck and strategy, and conservationists had done their best to guess which ones might hit it off. They noticed that marmots who hibernate in the same burrow tend to be good chums by the time they wake up, and that's exactly what happened with Sally and Pepsi. Born in captivity, the couple were later released in a protected wilderness area with their pups, where they are all enjoying freedom for the first time in their lives.

SCARFACE BLACK-FOOTED FERRET

When a ranch dog in Wyoming caught a black-footed ferret in 1981, scientists were elated to learn that the bandit-masked creatures still existed – they had feared they were extinct. But it wasn't long before the species was really struggling. The only way to save them was to round up all 18 remaining ferrets, one of the rarest mammals on earth at the time, and start a captive breeding programme. They managed to get 17, but the ferrets failed to reproduce. Conservationists' only hope was to find the last male holdout, a wily critter known as Scarface. It took several months but Scarface was finally captured and went on to father many offspring. He died in 1992 but lives on through his descendants and is credited as the heroic saviour of his species.

THE BOSS GRIZZLY BEAR

The biggest, toughest grizzly in all of Canada is known as The Boss. He's made headlines for strolling through a popular picnic area in broad daylight, giving hikers quite a scare. The Boss's tracking collar provided valuable data to scientists about his massive range. During his first year wearing the device, he covered more than 2,500 square kilometres (almost 1,000 square miles), often coming dangerously close to railway tracks and highways. He's even survived being hit by a train! The Boss's tracker stopped working in 2013, but people still report sightings of him. He's remarkably relaxed around humans – maybe a bit too relaxed. Once, when hikers stumbled across the massive bear munching on a carcass, he merely let out an annoyed huff and kept on eating.

NORTH AND CENTRAL AMERICAN WILDLIFE WINS

The modern wildlife conservation movement started in America and has had a number of successes over the years:

- 🐾 The American alligator was recognized as an endangered species in 1967. Authorities cracked down on gator hunting and the species made a full recovery within 20 years.

- 🐾 Generations ago, there were tens of millions of bison roaming the American plains. Hunting – for food, sport and other reasons – brought the bison close to extinction. People even amused themselves by shooting at them from passing trains! After conservation action, American bison numbers are back to hundreds of thousands.

- 🐾 Researchers hope to alter the DNA of the black-footed ferret to make them more resistant to a deadly disease – the sylvatic plague – which nearly wiped them out years ago.

- 🐾 Channel Island foxes live only on six islands off the west coast of America. The species was saved from extinction within just 12 years thanks to a captive breeding programme. It's the fastest recovery of any animal once listed as an endangered species.

- 🐾 California condors were so close to dying out four decades ago,

there were only 23 left in the wild. So scientists did something very bold – they captured all the remaining birds and started a successful breeding programme. Now there are almost 300 condors flying free.

❧ New fencing along public roads in south-west Florida, USA, are keeping Florida panthers safe from cars and other vehicles. There were fewer than 20 panthers left in the 1970s, but their numbers have slowly grown to about 200.

❧ The Frozen Zoo – a facility at San Diego Zoo in California, USA – stores the DNA of more than 1,000 species. These precious cells are like a space-age Noah's Ark! Using this DNA could save entire species one day.

❧ Decades of bounty hunting reduced the number of grey wolves so dramatically that barely any remained in the "lower 48" US states (the United States without Alaska and Hawaii). The Endangered Species Act gave the wolves legal protections and today 6,000 thrive in the wild.

❧ Grizzly bears in Yellowstone National Park in Wyoming, USA, have come a long way since 1975, when there were only 136 living there. Now over 700 grizzlies call the park home.

❧ A mountain lion in California's Santa Monica Mountains, P-54, gave birth to three kittens in 2020. The father, P-63, crossed a busy freeway to reach her from another area, bringing much-needed genetic diversity to the region's declining mountain lion population.

OTHER AMAZING NORTH AND CENTRAL AMERICAN ANIMALS

A grizzly bear known as **399** lives in Yellowstone Park in the US and is one of the oldest known grizzlies outside a zoo. She's produced 22 cubs (including rare quadruplets!). 399 and her many grand-cubs have a devoted fan club.

A Mexican red-kneed tarantula named **BELINDA** was a familiar sight on TV in the 1990s and appeared in the film *Indiana Jones and the Temple of Doom*, alongside actor Harrison Ford. Belinda was also used in hypnotherapy sessions to help people overcome their fear of spiders.

JOY was a sea otter who served as a surrogate mother for orphaned sea otter pups at the Monterey Bay Aquarium in California, USA. The staff nicknamed her "Super Mom"!

In the 1890s, **LOBO** – the legendary leader of a band of wolves in New Mexico, USA – seemed to have survival superpowers, able to avoid any trap set for him. The battle of wits between Lobo and a determined bounty hunter raised the awareness of wolf hunting in the wildlife conservation movement.

MAYKE is a Belgian Malinois who flunked out as a drug detection dog and went on to become a top-notch conservation dog. He's trained to detect jaguar and ocelot scat in the south-west US.

Red-tailed hawks usually nest on cliffs and rock faces in the wild, but in New York City, they build their homes atop tall buildings. A light-coloured bird called **PALE MALE** was the most famous hawk to do this. He lived high above posh Fifth Avenue and fathered about 30 chicks.

In 2005, blue iguanas were all but extinct in the wild on the Caribbean island of Grand Cayman, the only place they lived. An iguana called **PETER** is an enthusiastic ambassador for the breeding programme that has saved these reptiles. He's even met British royalty – the Prince of Wales patted him on the head!

The ancestors of a mustang called **PICASSO** were horses that came to America with Spanish explorers in the sixteenth century and escaped. This means Picasso is considered feral, not wild, and therefore is not protected by conservation laws. His incredible survival skills have become a legend over the course of his long life, inspiring paintings, poems and songs.

Two male birds at Chicago's Lincoln Park Zoo are part of a managed breeding programme. They are the first critically endangered **PUERTO RICAN PARROTS** to live in the continental United States.

WINNIE-THE-POOH was inspired by a real-life bear who belonged to a Canadian soldier. Winnie was a troop mascot who went to live at London Zoo during World War Two. Two of his biggest fans were a little boy named Christopher Robin and his father, the author A. A. Milne.

ENDANGERE

VULNERABLE

EXTINCT

SOUTH AMERICA

The Amazon rainforest is the largest rainforest in the world, a dense, gigantic wilderness that stretches across nine South American countries. It's home to a mind-boggling array of mammals, birds, reptiles and amphibians, and scientists discover a new species there every other day. There are untold numbers of tropical plants and animals yet to be discovered.

Known as "the lungs of the planet", the Amazon is facing a growing threat from deforestation. This is when trees are cut down to make space for farms, crops, cattle ranches and new buildings. Huge swathes of rainforest are chopped down and burned each day. When the fires get out of control, as they did in 2019, it causes incredible devastation to wildlife.

In the 2011 animated film *Rio*, the last male Spix's macaw journeys to South America to find the last female of his species. In real life, the beautiful birds that inspired the film were already believed to be extinct, never to be seen again. Or were they? In 2016, a teenage girl in Brazil spied one in her family's garden and managed to capture it on film. News of this unexpected sighting of a Spix's macaw thrilled birdwatchers across the globe.

At the rate they're disappearing, South America's awe-inspiring rainforests and all the marvellous creatures in them, like the Spix's macaw, may be completely gone within a hundred years. We need to take action now if we hope to save this country's extraordinary treasure trove of wildlife!

CAPLIN ROUS CAPYBARA

Caplin Rous was one of the world's best-known capybaras. The second part of his name, pronounced like "rose", stood for Rodent of Unusual Size (a reference from the movie *The Princess Bride*). He was definitely a big boy, and with his barrel-shaped body, shaggy hair and cute beaver-like face, people often mistook him for a giant hamster. Capybaras hail from South America but Caplin lived in Texas, USA, where he was a local celebrity and had thousands of followers on social media. He loved fruit ice lollies, splashing about in a pool and meeting his fans, and he was guaranteed to draw a crowd wherever he went. He often accompanied his human mum on school and library visits and inspired her to start the ROUS Foundation, which is dedicated to capybara conservation.

DIEGO GIANT TORTOISE

Diego is credited with helping to save his species in the Galápagos Islands.
A desperate captive breeding programme started there in 1965 when there were
only 14 giant tortoises left. Diego had been living at San Diego Zoo in the US for
several decades but returned to his birthplace for a truly life-or-death mission –
making babies, which he did with great success for the next 44 years. There are
2,000 Española giant tortoises in the Galápagos today and Diego fathered about
800 of them. Another tortoise, E5, fathered even more, but Diego's colourful
personality attracted a greater share of fame and media attention. Now more
than a century old, Diego and the other 14 original breeding adults have been
released into the wild for a well-earned retirement.

KARINA GIANT OTTER

Giant otters are endangered in their native South American habitat but Karina lives in Alabama, USA, where she has a special bond with a zookeeper called Dane. Karina's curious and quirky personality was evident right from the start. Whenever she gets new enrichment toys, she's determined to figure out how they work. Clever Karina has also mastered 70 challenges, including running through tubes, playing fetch and dunking a ball through a mini basketball hoop. The training keeps Karina's brain and body in top form and boosts her confidence, things that are very important for wild animals living in zoos, which can be rather stressful. Karina's ground-breaking work is being shared with zoo experts worldwide to help improve the lives of other animals in captivity.

MAYA JAGUAR

Maya arrived at the Big Cat Sanctuary in England when she was five days old and needed round-the-clock care. The boisterous youngster was totally black, a rare genetic mutation for a jaguar, and she had been rejected by her mum. One month later, Maya was eating solids and teething, but her legs seemed wobbly and her eyesight wasn't quite right. Experts suspected that her brain and nervous system weren't working properly and ordered a brain scan, making Maya the first jaguar ever to have an MRI. Regular exercise sessions in a swimming pool helped build up her muscles and retrain her nervous system, and today she's as fit and healthy as can be. She starred in a 2018 TV docuseries called *Big Cats About the House*, which introduced scores of people to her species, helping to raise money for jaguar projects at the University of Costa Rica.

MISS BAKER SQUIRREL MONKEY

Miss Baker was born in Peru and was one of two primates selected for the American space training programme. In 1959, she and a monkey named Able embarked on a history-making 15-minute suborbital flight that included nine minutes of weightlessness. They were the first mammals to fly in space and make it back home alive – an experiment that many now consider inhumane. Miss Baker charmed everyone at a post-flight press conference, munching on peanuts as reporters and photographers jostled each other to get closer. She lived to be 27, the oldest known squirrel monkey in the world, and her brave contribution to science should never be forgotten. Today, at the US Space and Rocket Center in Alabama, visitors often leave a banana on the plucky space heroine's grave.

PAULA SLOTH

Paula is the world's oldest known two-toed sloth. Born in a tropical rainforest in South America, she now lives at Germany's Halle Zoo, where she was mistakenly believed to be a boy for 20 years. The truth finally came out when Paula went in for an ultrasound scan. Sloths usually live about 20 years in the wild and up to twice that long in captivity, but none have ever lived as long as Paula. She set a Guinness World Record in 2019 when she reached the age of 50, which is equal to about 90 in human years. What's the secret to Paula's incredible longevity? It might be her stress-free life and devoted caregivers, some of whom have looked after her for more than 30 years. Or maybe it's that Paula loves her role as a super slow-moving ambassador for her species!

PONCHO MACAW

Poncho used to work for a company that provided Hollywood studios with talented animal actors for films. The green-winged macaw shared the silver screen with stars like Jim Carrey, Eddie Murphy and Glenn Close, and she played roles in *Ace Ventura: Pet Detective*, *Doctor Dolittle* and *102 Dalmatians*. Quite a glamorous life compared to macaws in the wild, which are threatened with habitat loss and extinction. Clever and colourful Poncho retired from show biz in 2000 and moved to a farm in England, where she lives with the owner of an exotic pet shop. She's still a diva, refusing to fly and making a fuss if people don't pay enough attention to her. When Poncho turned 90 years old in 2015, she set a Guinness World Record as the oldest known parrot on the planet.

ROMEO AND JULIET SEHUENCAS WATER FROGS

Biologists in Bolivia captured a rare Sehuencas water frog in 2009 and named him Romeo. Their goal was to start a breeding programme, but no other frogs of his kind could be found. Poor Romeo lived by himself in an aquarium for years, so lonely that he stopped singing his mating song. Desperate to find him a companion, his caregivers posted his profile on an online dating site. The profile linked to a donation page that raised funds for an expedition to search for other frogs. In 2019, the team was elated to find a female frog they called Juliet. Romeo serenaded Juliet with his special song on their first "date" and the celebrity couple now share the same tank. Only four others of this species are known to exist, and scientists hope to see tadpoles someday soon!

SOUTH AMERICAN WILDLIFE WINS

There are all kinds of exciting conservation programmes currently underway in South America. Here are a few highlights:

- The blue-throated hillstar hummingbird, with its emerald and sapphire colouring, was only discovered in 2017. The tiny bird's natural habitat is equally tiny – just a 114-square-kilometre (45-square-mile) area of Ecuador. Conservationists are working to obtain legal protection for this area.

- Rewilding efforts in the Galápagos Islands include ousting invasive species and reintroducing native ones. Authorities have also set limits on the number of visitors each day to help keep the environment as natural and damage-free as possible. Visitors are required to stay two metres (six feet) away from wild animals too.

- A forested wildlife crossing for golden lion tamarins is under construction over a major highway in Brazil. Conservationists convinced the highway construction company to build and pay for the overpass, which will be the first of its kind in this country and link areas of rainforest to help these monkeys move around.

🐾 Ninety per cent of the world's jaguars live in the Amazon river basin, where they are losing their jungle habitat at an alarming rate. Concerned scientists are creating a network of protected areas spanning eleven South American countries. Linking their fragmented territories with these wildlife "corridors" will help the cats find mates and keep their population stable.

🐾 Peru passed a new law in 2018 that put limits on single-use plastic and banned all plastic items in vulnerable places, such as beaches, historic sites and protected wildlife habitats.

🐾 A number of cattle ranches in Bolivia have been converted to wildlife sanctuaries, with former farmers now working as tour guides.

🐾 The Mindo harlequin toad, last seen in Ecuador in 1989, was rediscovered 30 years later. The tiny frog was thought to be extinct, feared lost to an amphibian-killing fungus. Not only was the rediscovery a wonderful surprise, but scientists hope it might mean the toad has become immune to the disease.

🐾 Actor and climate activist Leonardo DiCaprio raised £4 million (nearly $5 million) to help fight fires in Brazil's Amazon rainforest in 2019. His foundation, Earth Alliance, donated the funds to five local organizations that battled the blazes.

OTHER AMAZING SOUTH AMERICAN ANIMALS

Belfast Zoo in Northern Ireland welcomed a baby vicuña named **BLUEBELL** in 2019. She lives with her parents **GRETCHEN** and **OZZY** and two other vicuña, a South American species related to camels that is dependent on breeding programmes to increase its numbers.

During the Covid-19 lockdown in early 2020, **CHICO** a Linnaeus's two-toed sloth, native to the forests of South America, went on a tour of an aquarium in Texas, USA, part of an enrichment programme for zoo animals. A trio of dolphins were so over-joyed by their odd-looking visitor, one of them attempted an upside-down sloth impression!

A South American Magellanic penguin named **DINDIM** has a human for a best friend. The man rescued the injured animal years ago off the coast of Rio de Janeiro. Dindim swims out to sea whenever he feels like it, but often returns and honks with delight when he spots his buddy.

A female **FERNANDINA GIANT TORTOISE** was found in the Galápagos Islands in 2019, taking conservationists completely by surprise. Her species hadn't been seen since 1906! Even at 100 years old, she may be able to help increase her species as 100 isn't that old for a giant tortoise!

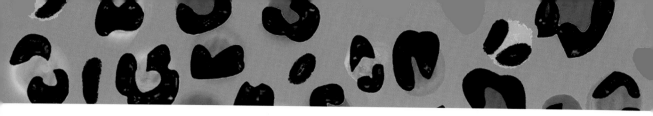

Jaguar cubs **JURUNA** and **MARINA** were the first of their kind to be reintroduced to the wild in 2019 in Argentina, a country where the big cats were once hunted almost to extinction.

Tamarins are usually found in southern Central America through central South America. But in 2019, three cotton-top tamarin babies were born to parents **LILO** and **KEVIN** at John Ball Zoo in Michigan, USA. Triplets in this rare species are almost unknown and Lilo and Kevin are already making a big contribution to the zoo's breeding programme. These primates have bushy white hair around their heads that makes them look like Albert Einstein!

LONESOME GEORGE was a Pinta Island tortoise who was the last of his species. In his final years, he was considered the rarest creature on earth and a symbol for wildlife conservation around the world. When he died in 2012, his entire species died out too.

Chilean flamingoes **POPCORN** and **PEANUT** were born at Belfast Zoo in 2019 and they were the first chicks to successfully hatch there. Zookeepers had finally resorted to using artificial nests and fake eggs to encourage breeding, a strategy that worked like a charm!

TIETA the toucan was missing half of her upper beak after being badly abused by wildlife smugglers. In 2015, researchers in Brazil created a new beak for her using a 3D printer. Tieta now works to raise awareness about animal trafficking.

ENDANGERED

VULNERABLE

EXTINCT

OCEANS OF THE WORLD

Our oceans are filled with hundreds of thousands of amazing marine species. Some are well known, while others lurk unseen and undiscovered in the darkest depths. One thing they have in common is that they're all increasingly threatened by human pollution.

Much of the rubbish we throw away ends up in our environment, poisoning habitats and harming wildlife. Plastic has been found in nearly every part of the world, even in the deepest trenches of the ocean. There, plastic waste is broken down by waves and sunlight into a microplastic "soup". These tiny particles are seriously bad for birds, turtles and other animals who mistake them for food.

In 2020, a whale washed ashore in Scotland with a 100-kilogram (220-pound) "litter ball" in its stomach. The mass of rubbish contained things like fishing nets, rope, plastic cups and bags. The poor creature died a victim of pollution, as do many sea birds and other marine animals each year.

Ocean pollution has inspired many young people to embrace eco-activism, including Greta Thunberg. When she first heard about the Great Pacific Garbage Patch – an enormous expanse of rubbish swirling around in the ocean – she was so upset that she became a passionate environmentalist. Another teenager, Dutch inventor Boyan Slat, created a huge rubbish-collecting machine that began working in the Pacific in 2019.

All the marine animals featured in this section are at risk because of pollution. That's why we all need to take action, in whatever way we can. If we don't, our oceans will someday contain more plastic than living things.

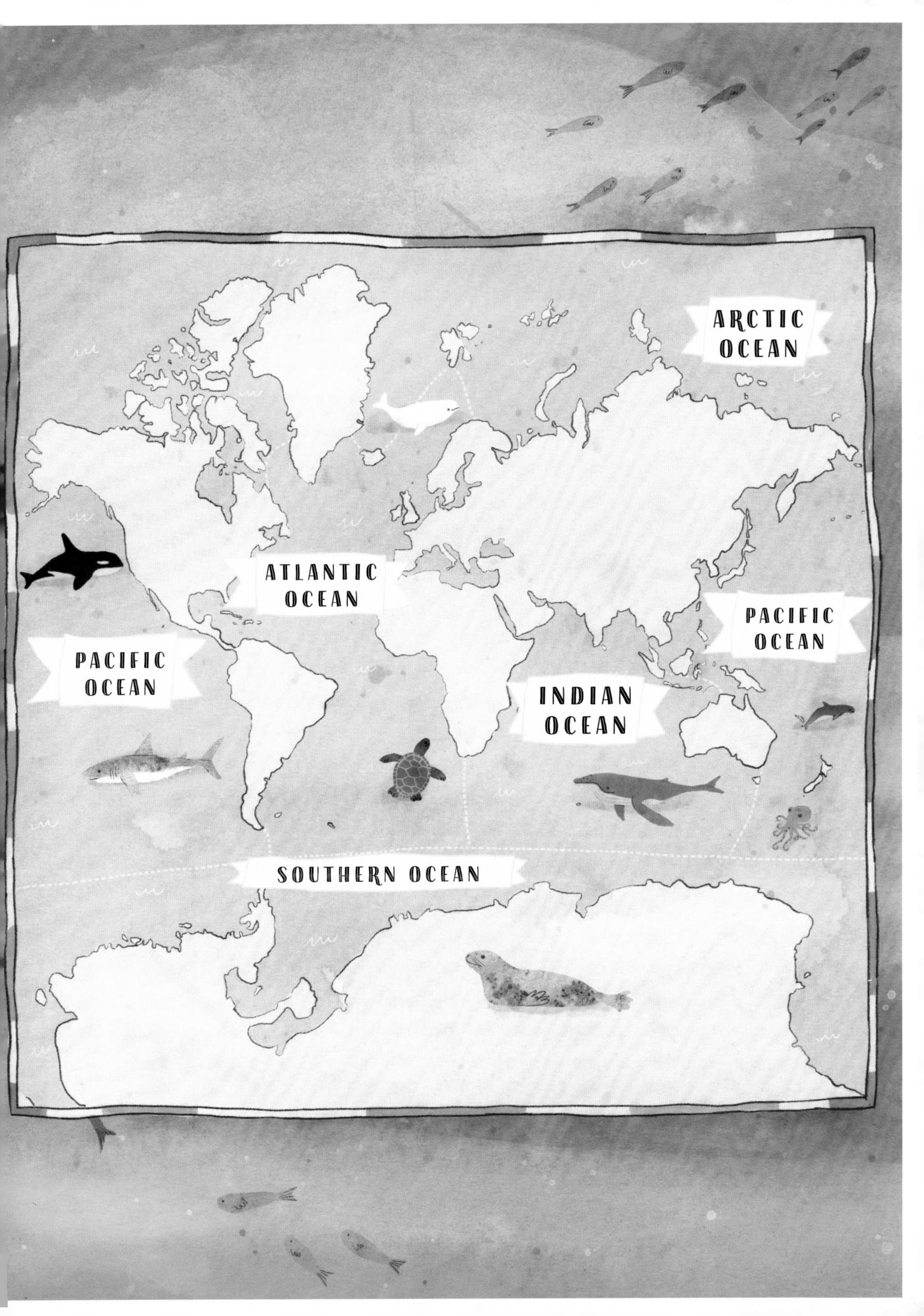

ARCTIC OCEAN

ATLANTIC OCEAN

PACIFIC OCEAN

PACIFIC OCEAN

INDIAN OCEAN

SOUTHERN OCEAN

DEEP BLUE GREAT WHITE SHARK

Deep Blue is a big girl, the largest shark ever known, weighing 2.7 tonnes (6,000 pounds) and stretching six metres (20 feet) long. Biologists attached a tracking device to her in Mexican waters in 2013, when the massive predator was being filmed for a Shark Week documentary on the Discovery Channel. Deep Blue was spotted again six years later near the Hawaiian Islands, where divers saw her feasting on a dead whale – sort of a shark's version of an all-you-can-eat buffet! One of Deep Blue's top fans is marine biologist Ocean Ramsey, who once spent many hours swimming alongside the great white. She shared her jaw-dropping photos of this up-close encounter on Instagram, hoping to encourage others to appreciate the beauty and ecological importance of sharks.

HVALDIMIR BELUGA WHALE

Hvaldimir was first seen off the coast of Norway in April 2019. He became known for going up to boats looking for food, and footage of him playing catch with rugby fans went viral on social media. He also made headlines for retrieving a woman's mobile phone that fell in the water. Alone and hungry, Hvaldimir swam around and around, seeking food and attention. He was obviously used to humans, but where did he come from? One clue was the harness he wore, labelled "Equipment of Saint Petersburg" in English. This led to rumours that Hvaldimir was a Russian spy! Spy or not, he needed help, so researchers started feeding him and gradually encouraged him to hunt on his own. Hvaldimir headed towards open water that summer and has been healthy and free ever since.

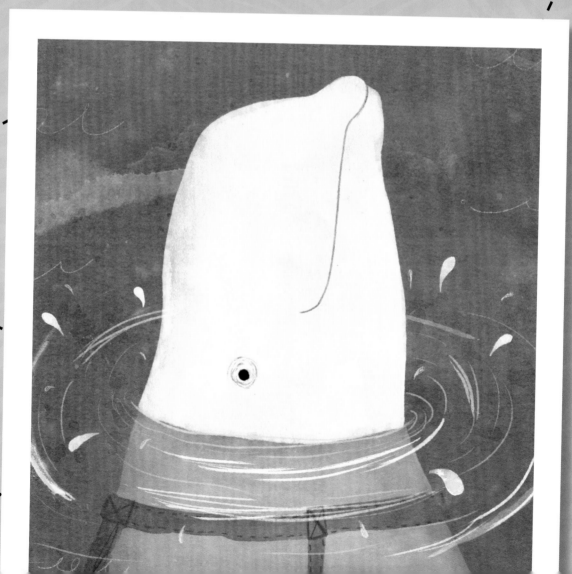

INKY OCTOPUS

Inky was brought to New Zealand's national aquarium by a fisherman in 2016. The rugby-ball-sized octopus was in rough shape, but the staff quickly realized that he was friendly and unusually intelligent. So intelligent, in fact, that he masterminded a daring midnight escape! He somehow broke out of his tank, slithered across the floor and made his way down a 50-metre (164-foot) drainpipe that led out to sea. When the staff came in the next day and found his tank empty, they were sad but not too surprised, as octopuses are known for their ability to solve puzzles and navigate complex mazes. Perhaps Inky was curious about what was going on in the outside world? Whatever his reason, one thing was certain – Inky had outsmarted the humans and was free once again.

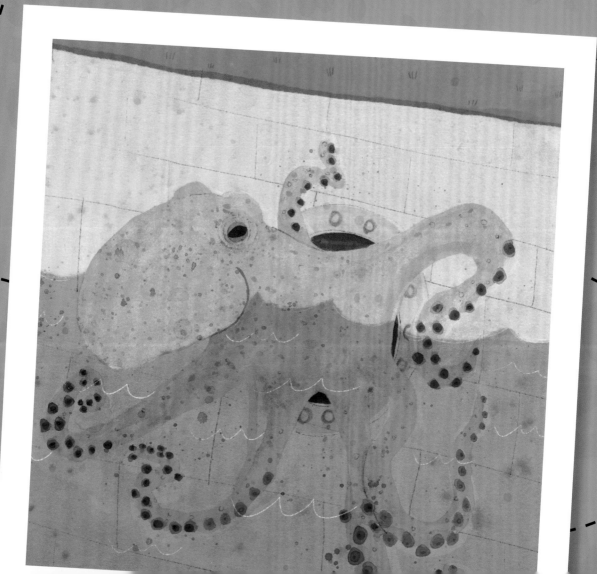

MIGALOO HUMPBACK WHALE

Migaloo is considered the most famous humpback in the world, and the only one that's an albino. He's been seen nearly every year in Australian waters since he was first spotted in 1991. Seven years later, researchers recorded him singing, something only male humpbacks do. People thought he deserved a proper name, so local aboriginal elders came up with Migaloo, which means "white fella". Migaloo is so easy to identify that researchers have gathered a great deal of data without ever having to tag him with a radio tracker. He tries to maintain a low profile, no easy thing when you're a massive white whale. Wherever the rare humpback goes, his devoted fans try to capture him with their cameras, posting their photos on Migaloo's social media fan pages.

PAUL'S SEAL LEOPARD SEAL

When photographer Paul Nicklen was in Antarctica shooting photos for *National Geographic* in 2009, he had an experience he will never forget. He came face to face with the largest leopard seal he'd ever seen, a species with a reputation for being ferocious. Things started off badly when the deadly predator took Paul's head and camera into her powerful mouth. This was a terrifying moment when he was totally at her mercy. But instead of harming him, the seal did something unimaginable – she started bringing him penguins. First live ones, then sickly ones and finally dead ones, even demonstrating how to eat them. Paul suspects that she figured he was rubbish at hunting and needed her help. A film of their incredible interaction later went viral on the internet.

PELORUS JACK DOLPHIN

Pelorus Jack was a Risso's dolphin who guided ships travelling between Wellington and Nelson in New Zealand. He was first noticed way back in 1888 and spent the next 24 years joyfully riding the bow waves of boats travelling from Pelorus Sound to the dangerously narrow French Pass, a journey of about eight kilometres (five miles). His fame grew over the years and he became a major tourist attraction, drawing the attention of such well-known figures as the American writer Mark Twain. Pelorus Jack was so beloved that his fans demanded – and won – legal protections for him in 1904. Mystery surrounds Pelorus Jack's death, but he most likely died of old age. His legend lives on with songs, a chocolate bar and even a Scottish country dance named in his honour.

SPRINGER ORCA

Springer became famous in 2002 when she was a malnourished orphan found swimming in Puget Sound, near the city of Seattle, USA. A close look at photographs and analysis of the sounds she made revealed that Springer was A73, a member of a dolphin pod located 402 kilometres (250 miles) north. Springer became a major news story as people debated about what to do with her. Scientists eventually agreed to capture the little orca and give her medical care and food. She was later transported to British Columbia, Canada and released near her family. Within weeks, Springer was seen travelling with the wild orcas and has stayed with them ever since, becoming a mum twice. This was the first time that a whale was successfully re-introduced to the wild after being cared for by humans.

YOSHI SEA TURTLE

Yoshi spent more than two decades in an aquarium in South Africa. But once the sea turtle was fully grown and old enough to breed, the decision was made to give Yoshi her freedom. Scientists spent 18 months getting Yoshi ready with a rigorous fitness programme designed to help her cope with rough ocean seas. Training sessions included swimming laps in her tank, with divers at each end giving her treats to encourage her to keep going. In 2017, at the age of 25, she was released into the ocean off Cape Town. All Yoshi's hard work paid off because she has since gone on to become the stuff of legend and is on track to set a new record for sea animal migration. In her first 26 months at sea, she travelled more than 37,000 kilometres (23,000 miles) – as far as the west coast of Australia – and she's still going!

OCEANS OF THE WORLD
WILDLIFE WINS

Scientists increasingly look to our oceans and their wildlife to gauge the health of the planet. Here are some positive developments:

- There are about 60 orcas in captivity around the world, but activists are working hard to free them. Keeping marine animals in cramped concrete pools to perform tricks is terribly cruel and animal "abusement parks" are now banned in many countries.

- The Belize Barrier Reef was threatened by overdevelopment and pollution until 2018 when the government banned oil and gas exploration in Belize's waters.

- The world's largest animals, blue whales, were spotted in "unprecedented numbers" in the waters around Antarctica in 2020, a sign the mammals might be staging a comeback.

- A 2018 ban on fishing nets in Abu Dhabi, United Arab Emirates, has reduced deaths of dugongs by more than half. Better known as sea cows, dugongs are related to manatees.

- Protections created by the Endangered Species Act helped save the Florida manatee from extinction in US waters. Young activists helped too, successfully campaigning to make the manatee the state marine mammal in 1975.

The fin whale population has doubled since the 1970s thanks to reduced catches in the North Atlantic and global bans on commercial whaling.

The Western South Atlantic humpback population has grown to 25,000 whales, an extraordinary recovery for the species. At one time there were as few as 450 left.

Australian scientists now use drones to keep an eye on endangered sea lions, which often live in remote regions. The drones take aerial photos that are used to determine the animals' health.

Up to one hundred million sharks are killed each year for their fins, which are used for shark-fin soup and in traditional Chinese medicine. One strategy to save them is eco-tourism, such as giving divers opportunities to swim with sharks.

Russia freed 10 orcas and 87 belugas from its "whale jail" in 2019. They were held captive there before being sold to aquariums and marine parks around the world.

Whale rescue teams in places like Canada's Bay of Fundy are made up of local fishermen who undergo special training and learn how to safely free whales caught in fishing lines and nets.

OTHER AMAZING OCEAN ANIMALS

In 2014, scientists in French Polynesia noticed a **BOTTLENOSE DOLPHIN** caring for a baby whale as well as her biological calf, something that had never been seen before. The baby whale stayed with his adoptive mum for almost three years before striking out on his own.

California surfer Todd Endris thought his life was over when he was struck three times by a great white shark in 2007. But a **POD OF DOLPHINS** formed a protective circle around him, allowing him to get to shore. He recovered from his injuries and said he owed his life to the dolphins.

In the late 1970s, staff at a Boston aquarium discovered that a harbour seal named **HOOVER** could say his own name and simple phrases such as "hello there". Hoover's remarkable ability to mimic human speech made him a hit with visitors and intrigued scientists for years.

Following the success of the movie *Free Willy*, activists campaigned to free the film's real-life star, a captive orca named **KEIKO**. He was moved to a sanctuary, where he learned to hold his breath longer, swim more and catch his own food. Keiko was eventually released near Iceland in 2002.

MILA the beluga whale saved the life of a Chinese diver in 2009. The woman was taking part in a free-diving contest amongst whales in a tank of water chilled to Arctic temperatures. Her legs cramped and she was in danger of drowning when Mila swam over and pushed her to the surface.

In 2008, two pygmy whales, a mum and her calf, beached themselves again and again on a sandbar in New Zealand. Luckily, a bottlenose dolphin named **MOKO** showed up and guided the whales back to open water.

NOC, a beluga whale who lived at an aquarium in San Diego, USA, for 30 years, was one of the first of his kind to mimic human speech. Noc told a human diver to get out of his tank by saying the word "out"!

OZY was the first octopus to unscrew a jar in under a minute. He set a new world record in 2014 while recovering from an injury at a New Zealand aquarium and was later returned to the sea.

WINTER is a bottlenose dolphin at an aquarium in Florida, USA, with a silicon and plastic prosthetic tail. Her story inspired the book and film *Dolphin Tale* and its sequel, *Dolphin Tale 2*.

FANTASTIC FACTS

ALBATROSSES have the longest wingspan of any bird on the planet.

ARCTIC FOXES live in dens that are sometimes used by many generations of foxes.

ARCTIC TERNS fiercely defend their nests, dive-bombing anyone who dares to come close.

BELUGA WHALES are able to swim backwards.

BISON can race up to 64 kph (40 mph) and have a two-metre (six-foot) vertical leap.

BLACK-FOOTED FERRETS are fossorial, meaning they live mostly underground.

BLACK ROBINS are all descended from a single bird, which makes them vulnerable to disease.

BLUE IGUANAS are one of the longest living lizards; the record is 69 years.

BLUE WHALES are the loudest animals on earth, with calls louder than a jet engine.

BOWHEAD WHALES can live over 200 years, the longest lifespan of any mammal.

BROWN BEARS can run as fast as 48 kph (30 mph), faster than sprinter Usain Bolt.

CALIFORNIA CONDORS have enormous wingspans that stretch up to three metres (ten feet).

CAMELS can go weeks without drinking water, drawing energy from fat stored in their humps.

CAPYBARAS can stay underwater for up to five minutes at a time.

CHIMPANZEES have complex emotions and laugh when tickled, just like humans do.

CROCODILES can live for months without food.

DOLPHINS call each other by "name", using a unique whistle to identify each other.

ELEPHANTS mourn and sometimes "bury" dead family members, covering them with branches.

EUROPEAN MINKS have webbed feet and can swim up to 30 metres (100 feet) underwater.

GIANT PANDAS will do handstands to get their urine scent as high up a tree trunk as possible.

GIANT TORTOISES won't outrun a hare but cover three kilometres (two miles) a day on average.

GIRAFFES are very social animals yet rarely make any kind of sound.

GORILLAS help plant trees by eating fruit and pooping out the seeds as they roam about.

GREAT WHITE SHARKS have skin covered with tiny scales that are somewhat similar to teeth.

HEDGEHOGS were voted Great Britain's favourite mammal in 2016.

HIPPOPOTAMUSES are considered one of the most dangerous animals in Africa.

HUMPBACK WHALES can eat as much as 1,350 kilograms (nearly 3,000 lbs) of food a day.

JAGUARS that are completely black are known as black panthers.

KANGAROOS are the only large animal to use hopping as their primary means of getting around.

KOALAS have unique fingerprints, as do humans, gorillas and chimpanzees.

LEOPARD seals have only one predator, the orca.

LIONS are the only wild cats that live in groups, known as prides.

LYNXES aren't particularly fast, so they rely on surprise attacks to capture their prey.

MACAWS have tongues with a bone inside them, useful for tapping into fruits.

MARMOTS make loud whistles when alarmed, earning them the odd nickname "whistle pig".

MOOSE have antlers that can grow to almost two metres (six feet) long.

MOUNTAIN LIONS can't roar but they can purr, just like a pet cat.

NUMBATS can slurp up as many as 20,000 ants a day.

OCTOPUSES have three hearts, a large brain, eight "mini-brains" and blue blood.

ORANGUTANS are believed to be one of the most intelligent primates aside from humans.

ORCAS were once called "whale killers" and the two words got switched; they aren't whales at all.

PANGOLINS have super sticky tongues that are longer than their own bodies.

PENGUINS have knees.

PEREGRINE FALCONS are the world's fastest animals, diving at speeds of up to 320 kph (200 mph).

POLAR BEARS have black skin and translucent fur that reflects light so it appears white.

PRZEWALSKI'S HORSES are the only species of horse never to be domesticated.

PUFFINS were the inspiration for the cute porgs featured in the Star Wars movie *The Last Jedi*.

RED SQUIRRELS don't hibernate in the winter and rely on food that they've hidden away.

REINDEER can outrun an Olympian sprinter from the time they are one day old.

RHINO horns are made out of keratin, as are human hair and fingernails.

SAOLAS are so extremely shy that no one knew they even existed until 1992.

SCOTTISH WILDCATS are depicted on several Scottish clan crests.

SEA OTTERS often form attachments to certain stones and hang on to them for many years.

SEA TURTLES have been around since the time of dinosaurs, about 110 million years.

SEHUENCAS WATER FROGS love cold water and live in icy streams.

SLOTHS are the world's slowest mammal on land, but they are surprisingly good swimmers.

SNOW LEOPARDS are so shy and solitary there is no word to refer to a group of them.

SNOWY OWLS are diurnal as well as nocturnal, meaning they're active both day and night.

TASMANIAN DEVILS have big heads and small bodies, inspiring the Looney Tunes character Taz.

TIGERS can be identified by their personal barcodes; each one has a unique pattern of stripes.

WALLABIES look a lot like kangaroos but are much smaller and stockier.

WOLVERINES are fierce enough to chase away much larger animals, such as grizzly bears.

WOMBATS are the only animals on earth that produce cube-shaped poo.

TAKE ACTION

Here are a few things you can do to make life better for wild animals:

- Help educate others about wildlife by writing an article for a school newspaper or blog.

- Create a piece of art, take a photo or shoot a video that promotes wildlife conservation.

- Carry a reusable water bottle and a reusable shopping bag to avoid single-use plastic.

- Never buy any animal that belongs in the wild.

- Tell a trusted adult if you see any animal in trouble, such as living in inhumane conditions.

- Avoid places that harm or exploit wild animals, such as marine theme parks with orcas.

- Try to use "green" or eco-friendly products, such as sunscreen that won't harm coral reefs.

- Start a wildlife club at school to raise awareness about endangered species.

- Make sure party balloons don't "escape", as they can be harmful to wildlife.

- Learn more about wildlife by reading, doing research online or talking to an expert.

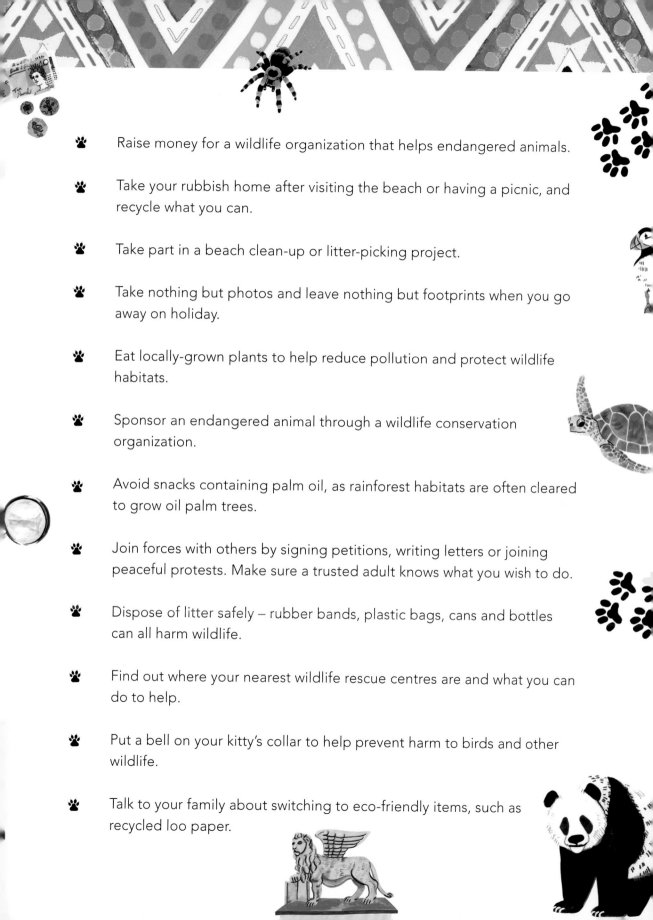

🐾   Raise money for a wildlife organization that helps endangered animals.

🐾   Take your rubbish home after visiting the beach or having a picnic, and recycle what you can.

🐾   Take part in a beach clean-up or litter-picking project.

🐾   Take nothing but photos and leave nothing but footprints when you go away on holiday.

🐾   Eat locally-grown plants to help reduce pollution and protect wildlife habitats.

🐾   Sponsor an endangered animal through a wildlife conservation organization.

🐾   Avoid snacks containing palm oil, as rainforest habitats are often cleared to grow oil palm trees.

🐾   Join forces with others by signing petitions, writing letters or joining peaceful protests. Make sure a trusted adult knows what you wish to do.

🐾   Dispose of litter safely – rubber bands, plastic bags, cans and bottles can all harm wildlife.

🐾   Find out where your nearest wildlife rescue centres are and what you can do to help.

🐾   Put a bell on your kitty's collar to help prevent harm to birds and other wildlife.

🐾   Talk to your family about switching to eco-friendly items, such as recycled loo paper.

GO WILD!
GOOD STUFF TO READ AND WATCH

If you want to know more about your favourite animals, here are some great books to consider. There are also some amazing TV series, movies and magazines listed on the next page.

BOOKS:

100 FACTS ENDANGERED ANIMALS – Steve Parker

AJAX THE KEA DOG – Corey Mosen

A WILD CHILD'S GUIDE TO ENDANGERED ANIMALS – Millie Marotta

A WOLF CALLED ROMEO – Nick Jans

AN ANTHOLOGY OF INTRIGUING ANIMALS – Ben Hoare

BORN FREE – Joy Adamson

ICE: CHILLING STORIES FROM A DISAPPEARING WORLD

ON THE ORIGIN OF SPECIES – Sabina Radeva

OUR PLANET – Matt Whyman and Richard Jones

RED ALERT! 15 ENDANGERED ANIMALS FIGHTING TO SURVIVE – Catherine Barr and Anne Wilson

THE GIRL WHO STOLE AN ELEPHANT – Nizrana Farook

THE SURPRISING LIVES OF ANIMALS – Anna Claybourne and Stef Murphy

WILDLIVES: 50 EXTRAORDINARY ANIMALS THAT MADE HISTORY – Ben Lerwill and Sarah Walsh

TV AND MOVIES:

BABY CHIMP RESCUE

BLUE PLANET

BORN FREE

DOLPHIN TALE

DOLPHIN TALE 2

ELEPHANT

FREE WILLY

MARCH OF THE PENGUINS

OUR PLANET

REINDEER FAMILY & ME (AND OTHER
DOCUMENTARIES BY GORDON BUCHANAN)

RIO

THE BLUE PLANET

THE LION KING

THE STORY OF THE WEEPING CAMEL

MAGAZINES:

ECO KIDS PLANET

NATIONAL GEOGRAPHIC KIDS

SCIENCE + NATURE

THE WEEK JUNIOR

GLOSSARY

ACTIVIST – a person who campaigns for some kind of social, political or environmental change

ADVOCATE – a person who speaks up on behalf of an animal or another person

AKA – short for "also known as"

ALBINO – an animal with little or no colouring

AMPHIBIAN – a cold-blooded vertebrate animal, such as a frog or a toad, that spends part of its life on land and part in water

ANIMAL WELFARE – an animal's physical and emotional needs, including companionship, food and shelter

ARTIFICIAL INSEMINATION – when sperm is put into a female to make her pregnant

ATMOSPHERE – a mixture of gases that surrounds the earth

BACTRIAN CAMEL – a camel with two humps

BIG FIVE – a term that refers to African lions, elephants, rhinos, leopards and Cape buffalo

BIODIVERSITY – the various plants and animals living in a certain area

BIOLOGIST – a scientist who studies living things

BOUNTY HUNTER – a person who kills a wild animal in order to collect a reward

BUSHMEAT – the meat from wildlife species that are hunted for human consumption

CAPTIVITY – keeping an animal in a cage, tank or other enclosure from which it can't escape

CARBON EMISSIONS – releasing carbon into the atmosphere, a major cause of climate change

CLIMATE – the average weather conditions in a particular place

CLIMATE CHANGE – changes in temperature and weather around the world that are increasingly caused by human activity, such as burning fossil fuels, farming and cutting down forests

CO_2 – short for carbon dioxide, a colourless and odourless gas

COLONY – a group of animals that live together, such as a colony of penguins

CONSERVATION – protecting nature and wildlife

CONSERVATIONIST – a person who works to protect nature and wildlife

CORAL REEFS – an underwater ecosystem characterized by reef-building corals

DEFORESTATION – when forests are cut down so land can be used for farms, roads, timber, etc.

DNA – a chemical inside the cells of all living things that contains important genetic information

ECO-FRIENDLY – something that doesn't harm wildlife or the environment

ECOSYSTEM – living things in a particular area that depend on each other in some way

ENDANGERED – a species at serious risk of dying out for ever

ENDANGERED SPECIES ACT – a law in the USA that protects animals in danger of becoming extinct

ENRICHMENT – toys, puzzles and other activities that enhance the lives of animals in captivity

EXPLOITATION – treating an animal or person unfairly in order to benefit from their work

EXTINCTION – when a species dies out completely

FERAL – an animal or species that was once domesticated or kept by humans but now lives in the wild or outdoors with little or no human contact

FREE DIVING – diving in deep water without any kind of breathing apparatus

GENE POOL – all the genes in a certain species

GENETIC DIVERSITY – the variety of genes in a particular gene pool

GLOBAL WARMING – an increase in temperature near the surface of the earth

GPS COLLAR/TRACKER – technology that uses the Global Positioning System (GPS) and allows scientists to remotely monitor a wild animal's movements

HABITAT – a place where an animal or plant lives in the wild

HABITAT LOSS – when a habitat is destroyed or is no longer able to support the plants, animals or other organisms that live in it

HIBERNATION – a long period of remaining inactive in the winter

HUMANE – to treat people or animals with kindness and compassion

INBREEDING – close relatives breeding with each other, making them susceptible to disease

INVASIVE SPECIES – a species that is not native to a specific place

IVF – short for "in vitro fertilization", meaning to fertilize an egg with sperm in a lab

JOEY – a baby koala or kangaroo

KM/H – short for kilometres per hour

LGBT+ – short for lesbian, gay, bisexual and transgender

MAMMAL – a warm-blooded animal that usually has hair or fur and produces milk for its young

MARSUPIAL – a mammal that gives birth to its young before they are fully developed; the babies continue to grow in a pouch on their mum's stomach

MATRIARCH – the female head of a family or tribe

MICROPLASTICS – tiny bits of plastic that can get inside animals or humans and harm them

MIGRATION – to move from one place to another, usually every year around the same time

MONITORING – to watch a situation carefully

MPH – short for miles per hour

MRI – a special scan that produces detailed images of a body's internal organs and structures

NATIVE – a person, plant or animal that is born in or comes from a particular place

NATURALIST – a person who studies plants and animals

NATURAL RESOURCES – things that come from nature, such as air, wood, wind energy or natural gas

NORTHERN LIGHTS – aka aurora borealis – shimmering, coloured lights that appear in the sky at northern latitudes

POACHING – illegally killing an animal for its body parts, such as a rhino for its horn

POLLUTION – harmful substances, such as plastic rubbish, that get into the soil, air or water

POPULATION – the number of people or animals living in a certain area

PREDATOR – an animal that hunts, kills and eats other animals

PRESERVE – to keep something as it is in order to prevent it from being damaged or destroyed

PREY – an animal that is hunted and killed by another animal for food

PRIMATE – a class of animal with flexible hands and feet, opposable thumbs (placed opposite the fingers) and a highly developed brain, such as lemurs, monkeys, apes and humans

PROSTHETIC – an artificial body part

RADIO COLLAR – aka radio tracker or radio transmitter – an electronic device that allows scientists to remotely monitor a wild animal's movements

RAINFOREST – a dense habitat with many plants and animals in an area with heavy rainfall

RANGER – someone who patrols a forest or other natural habitat

RECYCLE – to collect and reprocess a material so it can be used again as a new product

REPTILE – a class of animal with dry scaly skin that lays soft-shelled eggs on land, such as snakes, lizards, turtles and tortoises

REWILDING – to restore land to its natural state, reintroducing native plants and animals

SAFARI PARK – a protected area where wild animals live in the open and can be viewed from a vehicle

SANCTUARY – a safe, protected place

SCAT – wild-animal droppings

SPECIES – a type of plant, animal or other living thing

SUBORBITAL – travelling to outer space but not going around the earth

TREATY – an agreement between countries or peoples

TROPHY HUNTING – hunting wild animals for "sport" and to show off

TUSK – a long pointed tooth that sticks out from a closed mouth, such as an elephant's tusk

ULTRASOUND – a scan that uses sound waves to create images of what's inside a body

VEGETARIAN – someone who doesn't eat animals but eats animal products, such as eggs or milk

VIRAL VIDEO – a video that is widely shared online

VULNERABLE – a species that is likely to become endangered

WILDLIFE CROSSING – aka land bridge or animal bridge – a structure that gives animals a way to safely move through their natural habitat, avoiding busy roads, railway tracks or other hazards

WILDLIFE TRAFFICKING/SMUGGLING – illegally taking wild animals in or out of a country

ABOUT THE AUTHOR

KIMBERLIE HAMILTON is a writer who used to live in sunny Southern California and now lives in misty Northern Scotland with her partner John and four cats. She has written all sorts of things over the years, including screenplays, travel brochures and teaching materials for her English language students in Japan. She is passionate about animals and loves to write entertaining non-fiction books for young people with curious minds. Kimberlie has a Master's degree in Screenwriting from the University of California, Los Angeles and a Master's in Creative & Cultural Communication from the University of Aberdeen. She aspires to have her own sanctuary someday for cats and other animals in need of a loving, forever home.

KIMBERLIEHAMILTON.CO.UK

Also by Kimberlie:
REBEL CATS! BRAVE TALES OF FEISTY FELINES
REBEL DOGS! HEROIC TALES OF TRUSTY HOUNDS
GENERATION HOPE: YOU(TH) CAN MAKE A DIFFERENCE!

Kimberlie wishes to thank her feline companions, the California Cats, for their emotional support while writing this book.

SAMMY JO   ELSA   SCOUT

ABOUT THE ILLUSTRATORS

AARON CUSHLEY (COVER ILLUSTRATION)

Aaron is an illustrator and doodler of dogs and all sorts of other animals, people and places. From Belfast, he studied Illustration and Graphic design at Ulster University Belfast School of Art. Aaron's work stems from his inner child and the innocence and creativity that emerges when he takes a pencil in his hand.

EMMA JAYNE (PATTERNS, BORDERS AND ICONS)

Emma is an illustrator from the beautiful county of Cheshire, in the UK's North West. She likes to work both digitally and traditionally, usually starting off by painting with gouache, using ink and coloured pencils then finishing off in Photoshop. Emma enjoys finding her inspiration in nature, vintage fairs, films and through travelling around the UK and abroad on city breaks to parts of Europe.

JESTENIA SOUTHERLAND (ILLUSTRATIONS: AFRICA)

As the daughter of two Airforce veterans, Jestenia spent most of her childhood moving from place to place. Moving around has exposed her to a variety of people and places. From North Carolina, USA to Germany and England, each was a valuable experience and had an effect on her growth as an artist. In her art she aims to portray a sense of whimsy through bright colours, graphic shapes and charming characters. She loves stories that trigger the imagination, and the potential of passing that feeling onto others is what drives her as an illustrator. When she's not drawing, she loves spending time with her two dogs, Kojack and Katia.

KIM EKDAHL (ILLUSTRATIONS: THE POLES)

Kim is a freelance illustrator based in Sweden. She has roots in game development and worked as a lead artist in the game industry before deciding to pursue illustration full time. Working with games made her realize her love for creating unique characters and telling enchanting stories with her art. When she's not illustrating, she enjoys playing games, reading fantasy or sci-fi novels and taking care of her plants, all of which are things that inspire her art greatly.

TSAI-YI HUANG (ILLUSTRATIONS: ASIA)

Tsai-Yi is a Taiwanese illustrator currently based in New York. She specializes in playful, sophisticated and whimsical styles. She loves using water media and digital painting to create the world she is imagining. Sketching strangers is one of her favourite things to do in coffee shops. She cares about many social issues, so creating illustrations that can influence people is one of her goals. Being an illustrator whose works can touch people and make a difference in the world is her life dream.

AMELIA HERBERTSON (ILLUSTRATIONS: AUSTRALIA)

Amelia is an illustrator based in Sydney, Australia. In her cosy, plant-filled studio, Amelia creates vibrant and colourful artworks inspired by her love of nature, botanicals and her collection of vintage children's books. Working primarily with watercolour and gouache, Amelia creates quirky illustrations featured on stationery and home décor. When she's not in the studio, Amelia can be found gardening, watching cheesy 80s movies or reading a book with a cup of tea.

STEPH MARSHALL (ILLUSTRATIONS: EUROPE)

Steph has been working as a freelance illustrator from her home studio in West Berkshire since she graduated from university in 2012. Her bright, playful illustrations are created using a mixture of Photoshop and hand rendered textures. She loves to incorporate elements of pattern within her work, and has a particular fascination with maps. Her work is often inspired by her adventures around the world and people from the different cultures that she meets on the way.

STEPHANIE FIZER COLEMAN (ILLUSTRATIONS: NORTH AMERICA)

From a young age, Stephanie Fizer Coleman dreamed of a creative career, although she imagined being a dancer or a choreographer, and couldn't have fathomed the twisty path that would lead her to be an illustrator. These days she can't imagine working at anything other than illustration. Steph works in Photoshop and thrives on creating beautiful, textural illustrations of her furry and feathered friends. Having grown up in a rural area, she is inspired by nature in all its grandeur. Steph lives in West Virginia with her husband and two dogs.

JULIANA MOTZKO (ILLUSTRATIONS: SOUTH AMERICA)

Juliana is a Brazilian illustrator who has loved drawing and painting ever since she was a little girl. She's fascinated about pets and children's books, and she loves to create cute artwork that touches people's hearts. After graduating in Arts and Pedagogy, she worked as an art teacher and pedagogical coordinator for almost 10 years before becoming a freelance illustrator.

KATIE WILSON (ILLUSTRATIONS: OCEANS)

Katie lives and works in a little old railway house on the beautiful South Island of New Zealand. She creates for both adults and children and her illustrations are sweet and cheerful with a handmade feel. When she isn't drawing she can be found walking the dog, hanging out with a horse or planting fruit trees in the garden.

INDEX